STEVE ANKERS is a Liverp the role of expatriate, opinio has co-authored two satiric; the semi-mythical conurbati *It's a Dog's Life for the Other* a vet. He worries about his car size of the Toblerone bar and LIVERPOOL's habit of conceding goals from set pieces.

Follow Steve at: sankersblog.wordpress.com

Praise for Northern Soles

This delightful road trip from Liverpool to Hull takes us along the way through history and present day, from industrial revolution to good works, art works, environmental wonders and remarkable people. Exploring multitudes of unknown highways and byways, Steve Ankers' journey bristles with insights into how we live now and how history shapes our present and our future.
Polly Toynbee, Journalist and writer on social affairs

...a wisecracking travelogue, liberally peppered with British rain, bunions and endlessly curious factoids from the recipe of 'blind scouse' to how Adam Ant found his stage name in a Liverpool urinal.
Mark Elliott, British travel writer

I so enjoyed this witty, somewhat serendipitous adventure led by our guide from Liverpool to Hull; and enriched by memories, encounters with stalwarts of the voluntary sector that is the beating heart of England, and enlivened by the truth that walking in the countryside isn't always the sublime experience it's cracked up to be. Do read it.
Fiona Reynolds, Environmental campaigner and writer

NORTHERN SOLES

A COAST TO COAST WALK

STEVE ANKERS

SilverWood

Published in 2018 by SilverWood Books

SilverWood Books Ltd
14 Small Street, Bristol, BS1 1DE, United Kingdom
www.silverwoodbooks.co.uk

Copyright © Steve Ankers 2018
Map © Claire Horsman 2018

The right of Steve Ankers to be identified as the author of this work
has been asserted in accordance with the Copyright, Designs
and Patents Act 1988 Sections 77 and 78.

Text reproduced from *Pevsner Guide to Manchester* © Yale 2002|
'Friday Night at the Royal Station Hotel' © Faber and Faber 1966 |
Crap Towns: The 50 Worst Places to Live in the UK © Boxtree 2003

ISBN 978-1-78132-756-2 (paperback)
ISBN 978-1-78132-795-1 (ebook)

British Library Cataloguing in Publication Data
A CIP catalogue record for this book is available from the British Library

Page design and typesetting by SilverWood Books
Printed on responsibly sourced paper

To the charity volunteers and staff striving to save the social and environmental soul of your communities. The nation owes you thanks. To all of you this book is dedicated.

Contents

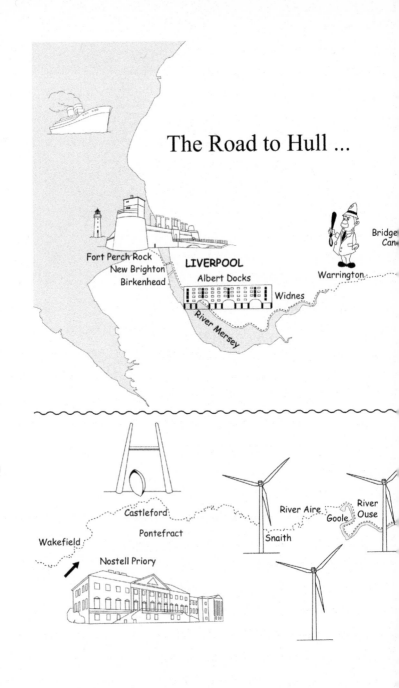

The Road to Hull ...

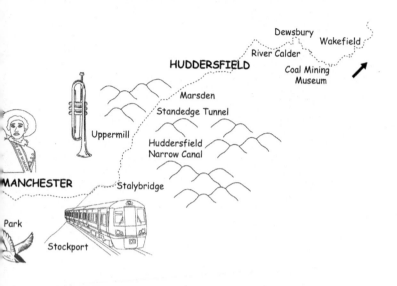

Dewsbury
Wakefield
River Calder
HUDDERSFIELD
Coal Mining
Museum
Marsden
Standedge Tunnel
Uppermill
Huddersfield
Narrow Canal
MANCHESTER
Stalybridge
Park
Stockport

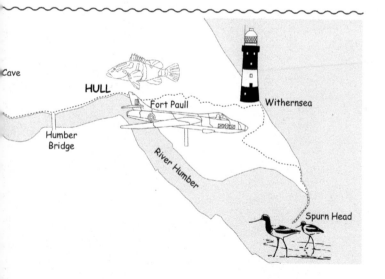

Cave
HULL
Fort Paull
Withernsea
Humber
Bridge
River Humber
Spurn Head

Chapter 1

Cannon Fire, Trippers and Roughs,
and a Ferry 'Cross the Mersey

"South America?"

    "No."

    "South America if I promised not to enjoy myself?"

    "No."

    "Syria?"

    "Probably not a good idea at the moment."

    Pause.

    "Where then?"

    "Anywhere you like. It's your trip."

    "Afghanistan? Congo? Elephant Island? Elephant and Castle? Chester Zoo?"

    "Now you're being silly."

    "Ok. How about I set off on a long walk somewhere and it's, like, really hard work and places you're not that bothered about?"

    "Well, I suppose, if it was somewhere that sounded a bit dull, so I wouldn't feel I was missing anything..."

Travel – or, at least, wandering about looking at stuff, scribbling something down, searching for places to eat and drink, then belatedly looking at the map to find out where I should have been – is in my blood. The head of the household, however, while supportive in principle, becomes a tad awkward at the prospect of me being away having a good time without her, especially if it sounds expensive. And that is how I come to be standing, on a cold blustery morning in early April in a fort built during the Napoleonic wars, about to embark on a two hundred mile walk through some of the less obviously scenic parts of England.

Where? One or two clues. My location has legitimately claimed at various times the largest theatre in England outside London, Britain's tallest building (what Blackpool has but higher), the largest outdoor swimming pool in Europe, Lily Langtry as its theatre's opening act, Elgar conducting his second performance of the Enigma Variations, no fewer than twenty-seven live performances by the Beatles and the Football League's oldest player.

I speak of course of New Brighton, on the corner of the Wirral peninsula facing Liverpool across the River Mersey as well as out to the Irish Sea. New Brighton and I go back a long way. When they bring out the film version of this book, it will now cut to black and white footage of two skinny boys scoffing their Fry's Five Boys chocolate bars ("Desperation, Pacification, Expectation, Acclamation, Realisation – It's Fry's", since you ask) while playing French cricket. One of those skinny boys was me. In those days I was so skinny that I had to hold onto my shorts while running around in order to remain decent; I don't have that problem now.

Some have written of their meanderings through Britain's most inspiring scenery, coast to coast via the Lake District or the Scottish Highlands. Others of traversing the country in a restored narrow boat. Me? I've opted to walk from Irish Sea to North Sea through post-industrial landscapes and city centres. I need the exercise. My wife points out that I've done so little walking in the past few years that I get out of breath changing TV channels.

I want to prove to myself that I'm up to a challenge. I've had some health issues and there's an orthopaedic surgeon in Brighton who will be deeply surprised if all of me makes it to the east coast. In gratitude for my treatment, I will be raising money for a health charity along the way. I want to explore parts of the country that normal family holidays can't do full justice to. Classic visitor attractions are fine, and I enjoy a good tea room like anyone else, but I have an over-developed interest in characterful old buildings and industrial archaeology, in things overlooked and the downright quirky. And I know there are brilliant environmental and charitable projects taking place in our communities. I want to find out more.

I'm fairly familiar with the northwest, having lived and worked there for nearly half my life, and this walk will enable me to dig beneath the surface. I'm much less familiar with the eastern end of my route, so plenty of new things to look forward to, and I know there are connections and similarities between Liverpool and Hull, the cities at either end of my trek, which I'm keen to explore.

But there are times when I wonder what possessed me. Funny how the memories of the pain and discomfort of previous long walks have faded over the years, permitting me to assume an innocent sense of optimism. They say this is what enables women to give birth more than once, or football supporters to turn up at the beginning of each season.

I plan to walk the whole thing and I intend to book myself into a variety of accommodation along the way. I won't be backpacking or dining out on harvested roots and nettles, scavenged chip wrappers or roadkill. This isn't Bear Grylls stuff – he can write his own book. Also, though much of my paid employment in the environmental sector is home based, I do have a job in Sussex that needs looking after, so I won't be doing the walk all in one go. I'm breaking it into half a dozen stages and hoping they don't notice I'm away.

Two hundred miles looked no more than an inch or two in

my *Reader's Digest World Atlas* but, now I'm on the starting blocks, as it were, I wonder if that twinge in my hamstring means that it would be wise to postpone. Just for five years or so. Writer Mark Wallingford, in *500 Mile Walkies*, admits that he set out on his epic dog-based hike along the South West Coast Path "to impress some girl I met at a party". I vaguely recall that when he eventually returned to London from his endeavours, she had no recollection of them having spoken. There's probably a moral to this story but I'm not sure what it is. So, why am I here? If I do go to any parties these days – which isn't often – I'm usually more interested in what there is to eat and getting home early than impressing anyone with my physical prowess.

Mrs. A has kindly supplied me with my very first pedometer which, she tells me, will measure the number of steps each day (does she suspect that I'll be hanging out in branches of Waterstones all day and hitching lifts?), how many calories I'm using, and the weather and time anywhere in the world. I'm not good with gadgets but I've agreed to give it a go.

How much stuff do I take? When I first went abroad hitch-hiking round Europe as a schoolboy in the 1960s, I was so worried about being away from home that I took a writing case with me – envelopes and everything. I was away nearly two weeks.

Nowadays I'm happy to reduce my baggage to the minimum if it's me that's going to carry it, and I try not to stand upwind of people after a few days. I read one travel writer who ripped out and discarded each page of the book he was reading once he'd read it – no point in carrying excess weight – though this isn't really an option for me as I invariably forget everything I've read by the next day and have to check back.

I came up on the train from Sussex yesterday. When Michael Portillo does his *Great Railway Journeys* I can't help but notice that his trains seem clean, comfortable, more or less empty and completely lacking in gurners doing rabbit ears behind him. My train wasn't like that. I did find it cheerfully nostalgic, though, hearing increasing numbers of Merseyside accents as we neared New Brighton, including the young lady in a hijab sat opposite who politely pretended to be interested in my plans.

This was my first time in New Brighton since playing pitch and putt and the odd arcade machine during holidays from university. I lived around here during two phases of my life: an early childhood outside Liverpool, near the Aintree racecourse; then a parental base in the Wirral while I lived and worked an hour away in Manchester. This time I arrived on a warm, sunny Sunday afternoon and the place was bustling with families and perhaps in better heart than I might have expected of a seaside resort well past its heyday. I headed over to see the location that I had chosen to start my walk on Monday and where I was due to have my own personal send-off in the form of – wait for it – cannon fire. Who would turn *that* down?

Fort Perch Rock stands at the very corner of the Wirral, the peninsula which juts out towards the Irish Sea between the rivers Mersey and Dee. Accommodating over 100 men and eighteen guns, the fort fired twice "in anger" at the onset of the First World War. A Norwegian sailing ship came up a channel that had been declared closed. Fortunately, the gunners – Territorials under the direction of the local dentist – had the wrong elevation and the shell flew over the ship, landing in Hightown on the other side of the Mersey. An irate householder collected the shell in a bucket and took it to the Merseyside Defence HQ and demanded an explanation. The shell was presented to the Seaforth Battery Commander whose officer placed it in the Mess Room, with the words, "A present from New Brighton".

The last guns were removed in 1954. (What happened in 1954 apart from the four-minute mile to stimulate this sudden outburst of recklessness? I see that in that year, President Dwight D. Eisenhower warned against the possibility of US involvement in Vietnam – I wonder how that turned out.) The fort was decommissioned soon after, passing through various hands until it was sold to the Darroch family, the current custodians, and is now home to maritime and aviation based museum displays, guest exhibitions and concerts.

Alongside an array of old Spitfire engines, I wandered through galleries depicting the radio room of the Titanic, Luftwaffe raids over Liverpool and the ill-fated Royal Navy submarine *Thetis* which sank on trials in Liverpool Bay in June 1939 with the loss of ninety-nine lives. The fate of the *Thetis* made an impression on my mother as a 20-year-old working in the city at that time, which is why its story was familiar to me.

I found Doug Darroch, who had kindly offered me my own cannon fire send-off, and we chatted through his family's connections with Perch Rock and my own recollections. Doug also pointed out to me, across the Mersey in Liverpool, various landmarks that I usually only see from close up: the football grounds at Anfield (Liverpool) and Goodison Park (Everton); the massive Titanic Hotel: and Liverpool's famous Pier Head waterfront. We agreed our start time for Monday morning and I left Doug closing up the fort for the evening.

By this time families were heading home, and a quietness settled over the resort. Not far from the fort, along the seaward end of the Wirral peninsula, I located the former site of another childhood memory; New Brighton's outdoor bathing pool. Opened in 1934, and said at the time to be the largest aquatic stadium in the world, it attracted 350,000 customers in its first three months, of whom 87,400 were bathers – which begs the question, what were all the others up to? I know you could expect a decent turnout to see a one-legged diver and there wasn't much on the telly in those days, but still…

From 1949 to 1989 the pool hosted the Miss New Brighton Bathing Girl Contest, won in its first year by Miss (I'm pretty sure they all had to be "Miss") Edna McFarlane, who won a princely £75, ceremoniously presented during a torrential downpour. But then, if she was already wearing her "swimmies", that shouldn't have been a problem. Storm damage in 1990 (makes a change from arson, I suppose, which I always assumed was the insurance claim of choice for outdated seaside structures) led to the pool's closure and it was demolished the following year.

I walked past the new shopping, hotel, entertainment and restaurant complex of Marine Point which now occupies the site of the old pool, but businesses were closing promptly at 6 p.m. as families departed, which created a rather downbeat atmosphere. The promotional video for the complex boasts, "And *best of all*, there's unlimited free parking". Mm. I guess London's West End can't compete with that. A wander round to the seaward side was bleak and unrewarding – it may not be easy to make flood protection works or the servicing areas of a Travelodge or Iceland store pretty, but hey.

To prevent me from ducking out of my great trek at the last minute, I'd arranged to be joined by three old friends from uni days for the first leg of the journey. Two of them, Keith and Peter, made it over from Liverpool to meet me in a New Brighton restaurant on the Sunday evening. We compared waist lines (burgeoning) and hair lines (less so) and unhelpfully provided actual answers to the conversational gambit, "How are you?" We each identified a range of ailments which would put us individually at a disadvantage on the walk on the following day. We agreed that technology is all very well, but you just can't beat a good solid map and we sought to identify as many towns as we could which had had more than one club drop out of the English Football League. (Here's one to start you off: New Brighton.) Yes, I know, it's a boy thing, but Keith's particularly good at it and I've known him a very long time...

My friends returned to Liverpool, promising to meet at Perch Rock in the morning. I headed for The Queen's Royal hotel in New Brighton for the night.

I wake in the morning feeling stiff in joint and muscle, which is, I suppose, par for the course on a walk of this length. Except that I haven't set off yet. The hotel wasn't able to provide breakfast for me but offered a discount for the inconvenience and pointed towards a nearby branch of Wetherspoons. I told the manager that I was walking to Hull, to which he – not unreasonably, and displaying a fine sense of geography – replied, "What, today?"

Like most seaside resorts, New Brighton doesn't look its best on this drizzly Monday morning as I head past the New Palace and Adventureland towards Perch Rock. Where yesterday afternoon there were families queuing for candy floss, ice creams and burgers, buzzing amusement arcades and shrieking children on funfair rides, the shops are shuttered below a splendid art deco frontage. The Wilkie family, *Purveyors of Merriment since 1912*, still own and operate the site – an impressive commitment in a world of ever-changing leisure.

I am meeting at Perch Rock with Peter, Keith and a third friend from student days, Lawrence. Doug, the owner, has laid on a photographer to record our departure. I find these days that photos don't really capture the essential me. Or perhaps they do, and I actually look like that. We gather round the old cannon on the battlements. It's pointing not out to sea but inland, in the general direction of Adventureland. I'm assuming this is so they can retrieve the cannon ball from the car park afterwards... But I learn that although there will be a big bang and smoke, I'm not to have a ball.

We need to press on. At a rough calculation, if it's taking a whole morning to leave Perch Rock, I should reach Hull around 2115 – and I don't mean quarter past nine. Doug fires the cannon, gives me the name and contact details of a friend who owns another Napoleonic fort near Hull – as you do – and off we go.

But first, I just want to cross over the road and give a hug to Sid who's sitting nicely outside the Floral Pavilion Theatre waiting for me. Actually, he's been sitting outside the theatre for seven or eight years and not complained once – being made of bronze. Sid is a black Labrador and marks the foundation in these parts of the Guide Dogs for the Blind.

Originating in Switzerland and the United States, the British element of this very worthy cause began when a Miss Muriel Crooke from Wallasey (of which New Brighton forms a part) and a Mrs. Rosamund Bond – both being German Shepherd enthusiasts – met up in London in September 1930 with American philanthropist, Mrs. Dorothy Leib Harrison Wood Eustis, who had set up her Seeing Eye scheme two years earlier in Nashville, Tennessee. Mrs. Harrison Eustis had, when living in Switzerland, bred German Shepherds as police dogs and become aware of a German guide dog training school for blind veterans of the First World War. (I have for this paragraph adopted the practice of indicating marital status as I suspect Mrs. Harrison Eustis would have expected no less.)

A trial scheme began in a lock-up garage in New Brighton with four German Shepherds in late summer the following year and when the owners of Judy, Flash, Folly and Meta finished their training in October, a trail had been blazed. In 1934, the Wallasey Corporation (in those days local authorities had reassuring names) provided The Cliff, an almost derelict house on the seashore, allowing the trainers, the owners and the dogs to be accommodated in one place for four weeks: still the basis of guide dog training. The Guide Dogs Association in this country now employs over a thousand people and there are nearly 5,000 guide dog owners in the UK. The Association is now based near Reading. But New Brighton has Sid.

Mrs. Harrison Eustis's legacy has been wide-ranging. Her work helped spawn guide dog schools around the world and paved the way for using service animals to help people with all kinds of disabilities. She is also credited with helping to change public attitudes towards the disabled and contributing to the disability rights movement that began in the 1970s.

I had wanted to begin my coast to coast on the shores of the River Mersey. Liverpool exists because of the Mersey. Its docks and the shipbuilders of Birkenhead brought business and employment on a mighty scale. It's not a pretty river but a majestic one. The very name speaks of hard grind. Lord Byron, as far as I'm aware, never tried to swim across it, though if he had, the local kids would have offered to mind his car while he was out of sight.

In a 1976 play, *Down the Dock Road*, Alan Bleasdale wrote a scene in which a gang of Liverpool dockers – obviously before the days of containerisation – accidentally let a crate of tinned food fall from a crane and into the river. "Oh well, at least there's salmon back in the Mersey," someone says. No single line that Liverpool born Bleasdale wrote then was more improbably prophetic than that joke. Salmon really are back in the Mersey and are caught as far upstream as Warrington.

While early plans for New Brighton envisaged a first class watering hole, a degree of degeneration set in and the place slid down the social scale. One Philip Sulley, describing the resort in 1889, wrote:

> Along the shore is a narrow, unsafe promenade…better known as 'Ham and Egg Terrace', the favourite resort of the Liverpool and Lancashire trippers and roughs… With more visitors and fewer trippers, New Brighton would be more flourishing.

The four of us are feeling right at home.

Leaving Sid, the Labrador behind, we can see ahead of us on the far side of the estuary the "Three Graces" of the Liverpool waterfront – iconic, listed, early 20th century office buildings – the Royal Liver, the Cunard and the Port of Liverpool. Something to aim for. Following the estuary upstream we pass the site of the New Brighton Tower, taken down for scrap in 1919, though the ballroom at its foot remained until destroyed in 1969 by – no surprises – fire. I have no strong childhood memories of the open-air pool. I only learned to swim in my thirties in Manchester with the aid of quantities of "swimming whisky" – you know, like they have cooking sherry which is cheap but fit for purpose; you're not going to waste good money on a single malt if you just want to relax enough to take your feet off the bottom. But I do remember the ballroom. Father Christmas, I recall, used it as his global operational base from the beginning of December and the walk through the fairy-lit grounds was something that no small boy should be expected to complete with dry pants.

The grounds featured at various times: a Japanese café; a Parisian tearoom; real live gondoliers and a lion house. The tower itself, along with its assembly hall, winter gardens, cycle track and massive ballroom, sported its own aviary and monkey house. The owners also established a professional New Brighton Tower Football Club in 1896. It was accepted into the Football League in 1898, played in front of average crowds of 1,000 in a stadium at the tower which could have held 80,000, and folded three years later. In 1921 a new club was formed, New Brighton, which graced the Football League without troubling the trophy inscribers, until 1951, primarily in Division 3 North.

New Brighton is full of things that are no longer there. As well as not seeing the open-air pool or the tower, we don't see either of the resort's piers as they were taken down in the 1970s. But we can see the *Black Pearl Pirate Ship* on the beach opposite the tower grounds. *The Pearl* is a nearly full-size, three masted man-of-war, constructed largely from salvaged materials and driftwood found on the beach. As well as being a children's play structure, it serves as a mock-up for RNLI exercises and hosts wedding ceremonies. Insert your own joke here about walking the plank, years of servitude, or hardtack containing the lesser of two weevils.

The promenade along the Wirral coast of the Mersey past pleasant housing and open spaces is easy walking, even for us. This proves an affable way of starting out the only accompanied part of my walk for a while. The Liverpool and Manchester stretches of the journey will be the most familiar to me and no doubt throw up the greatest number of opportunities for socialising on the way. I'm spoilt for choice when it comes to deciding my route, with so many places of interest in Birkenhead and all down the Wirral, or across the Lancashire plain, perhaps following the Liverpool to Leeds Canal past my first home near the Aintree (Grand National) racecourse. But I've opted to head into Liverpool city centre then follow off-road paths as much as possible to Manchester.

There have been ferries across the Mersey for a thousand years.

Monks from the Benedictine Priory in Birkenhead would row passengers across, which must have kept them fit. During the last century, ferries ran from Liverpool's Pier Head to various places on the Wirral but services to New Ferry and to Eastham (where the Manchester Ship Canal runs into the river) ended in the 1920s, to Rock Ferry in 1939 (shortly after the opening of the first Mersey tunnel), to Egremont in the Second World War and to New Brighton in 1971. In 1950 some 30 million passengers used the ferries: by 1970 this was down to 7 million. Passenger numbers continued to fall during the seventies, accentuated by the opening of the second road tunnel beneath the river in 1971, and the remaining services survived more for sentimental reasons than economic or practical. But major initiatives like the International Garden Festival in Liverpool in 1984 and the arrival of the Tall Ships race in the same year led to a recovery in the number of passengers.

At Egremont, we pass the site of one of the old ferry landing stages, now only recalled by the surviving Egremont Ferry Hotel. Only Seacombe (in Wallasey) and Woodside (for Birkenhead) now retain a ferry service to Liverpool, operating a triangular route primarily for holidaymakers, together with a limited commuter service. We are tempted to shorten the walk by taking the next ferry from Seacombe but decide that we are (just about) made of sterner stuff and press on for another mile and a half towards Woodside. For the last section, in order to reach the Woodside landing stage, we need to leave the shoreline and cross the "float", Birkenhead's extensive area of docks and shipyards developed from a large natural inlet. As in so many places, historic warehouses are being converted into apartments with enviable waterside views, at prices that prospective purchasers in the south east of England can only dream about.

I'm aware that Birkenhead would have been well worth a tarry.

It was referred to by my parents' generation as the 'one-eyed-city'. Explanations appear to range from dock riveters losing an eye in industrial accidents, to the streets being lit on one side only, to the locals turning a blind eye to pilfering in the docks... Dad said it was because the other eye was always looking down the Mersey tunnel towards Liverpool. My holiday jobs there contributed to the upkeep of the grass verges, the delivery of the Christmas post and the less than smooth operation of the labour exchange. Not the most glamorous of places these days, Birkenhead was famed in its time for having: the first scout group; Britain's first street tramway; and the world's first publicly funded park, created by Joseph Paxton and on which Frederick Olmsted based his ideas and designs for New York's Central Park.

When my parents lived there in the 1970s, economic decline and a lack of investment in public services meant that the once glamorous Birkenhead Park had become a sorry affair. In 1978, the Liverpool Daily Post stigmatised it as a refuge for "drunks and dossers" and in 1981 claimed that "pram mums" were avoiding the park for fear of being attacked – so, perhaps still a model for Central Park at that time. But, with the injection of Heritage Lottery, European and local funding, the noughties decade saw a major transformation including improvements to the paths, the planting of trees and shrubs, the cleaning out and reshaping of the lakes and the restoration of most of the Victorian features. As with so many of our public parks, however, the availability of funds for maintenance and management remains a major problem.

The Woodside ferry landing stage and passenger-bridge should look familiar, having featured in *Chariots of Fire*. The British athletes, including Eric Liddell, are in the process of embarking for France and the Olympic Games in Paris (sailing to France from Birkenhead smacks of really rubbish satnav, so I assume we were supposed to think it looked like Dover), when Liddell hears from a journalist that his heat for the 100 metres will take place on a Sunday, and the rest, as they say, is history. If Liddell had done his homework properly he could have saved himself a lot of bother, but the film would have been much shorter, with less boater throwing. Alas, it turns out that it's all new infrastructure at Woodside now and that bit of heritage has been and gone.

At least the ferry still runs, and provides the best way of arriving at what must surely rank amongst the great waterfronts, now part of the Liverpool Maritime Mercantile City UNESCO World Heritage Site. Of the "Three Graces" office buildings at the Pier Head, the most readily recognisable is the 1911 Grade I listed headquarters of the Royal Liver Friendly Society, one claimant to the title of Europe's first skyscraper. Its two clock towers are topped by two 18-foot-tall, copper Liver Birds. Believed by some to be cormorants, eagles to others, it is generally understood in Liverpool that the female bird looks out to sea, watching for the seamen to return safely home, while the male looks towards the city, to check when the pubs are open.

My mother was invariably seasick during the crossing (and suffered from claustrophobia in the Mersey tunnel, so she didn't get to Liverpool very often) but my father happily commuted to work on it for years. He told me – and I'm in no position to contest it – that commuters walked round the deck for their morning constitutional – all in the same direction, like you're supposed to do in the dodgems, and it was bad news for any interloper unaware of the etiquette.

The approach to the Pier Head is invariably marked on the ferry by loudly broadcast repetitions of Gerry and the Pacemakers' eponymous hit record. With the ferry operating through the summer months at 20-minute intervals, my current walking chum

Peter (occupying a corner office in the Liver Building for many years and more of a classical music fan himself), said the charm of this had begun to pall. Once more, and altogether now...

Chapter 2

Scouse, Slavery and Self-help

We've landed at the Liverpool waterfront and I'm looking forward to one or two days' exploration. While I claim the city as my first home, in truth my familiarity with the place over the years has been patchy. There are places I'm keen to revisit but I've also set my sights on a few locations that I'll be seeing for the first time – and in the company of friends. Peter and Lawrence are long established residents of Merseyside while for Keith this is more or less his first visit and we want him to be impressed.

We head for Ma Boyle's Alehouse & Eatery off the waterfront behind Liverpool's parish church of Our Lady and St. Nicholas, appropriately the patron saint of sailors. I check out the pub's lower bar and cellar as this means that I am now standing in what was for much of the 18th century part of a prison beneath a medieval fortified town house known as the Tower of Liverpool.

I'll be ordering the local speciality, scouse, for lunch. Scouse was a food staple before it became a dialect, much as words like, "Limey", "Kraut" or "Frog" have been used to define national stereotypes by their dietary habits. In its basic form, scouse is simply a mutton stew with vegetables – typically potatoes, carrots and onions – served with pickled beetroot or cabbage and bread. Unless it's near the end of the month and the household has run out of money, in which case you make do with "blind scouse", scouse without the meat. Mine is classic scouse and it tastes as good as I remember.

After lunch, we agree our arrangements for later in the day and to reach the waterfront I take Keith down Water Street to see some of the city's most striking historic buildings. Originally "Bonk Street" in the Lancashire dialect as it ran up the bonk, or bank of the river, it is one of Liverpool's oldest streets.

The town hall is Grade I listed and described in its listing as "one of the finest surviving 18th century town halls". Its Council Chamber, Hall of Remembrance and suite of lavishly decorated function rooms are closed to the public today, so we have to make do with the tiled and wood panelled entrance hall with its large wooden fireplace and murals depicting scenes from Liverpool's history, and the grand staircase hall and the cabinets holding the city's silver.

A few yards along is the Grade II* former Martins Bank HQ, completed in 1932, now empty but set to become the city's first five star hotel. This is also currently closed to the public, but a plea to the janitor that we have come all the way from the south of England just to catch a glimpse and will be really disappointed not to peek inside, happily proves enough to produce our own private viewing. With the city's financial history closely linked to Africa and the slave trade, it's disturbing, if not surprising, to see decorative panels depicting African children carrying bags of money. The top-lit banking hall has vaulted arcades, travertine walls, floor and columns and the original curved counter, light fittings and desks. Awesome. I hope I can afford to check into the hotel sometime.

Oriel Chambers, from 1864 and Grade I listed, was the world's first building to feature a metal-framed glass curtain wall. In contrast to the conventional buildings of the time with their smaller windows set into a brick or stone wall, the oriel windows, which became the defining feature, created an impression of a glass frontage and abundant light and set a precedent for so much of modern architecture. It did not trigger love at first sight. According to *The Builder* magazine of June 1866:

> The plainest brick warehouse in town is infinitely superior as a building to that large agglomeration of protruding plate-glass bubbles in Water Street termed Oriel Chambers. Did we not see this vast abortion – which would be depressing were it not ludicrous – with our own eyes, we should have doubted the possibility of its existence. Where and in what are their beauties supposed to lie?

I expect *The Builder* might have struggled with London's Shard.

We arrive at Albert Dock, without which no tourist can be said these days to have "done" Liverpool. Included, with the Pier Head, in the city's World Heritage Site, the largest collection of Grade I listed buildings in Britain date from 1846, have been restored and now accommodate restaurants, shops (admittedly mainly tourist tat), hotels, a branch of the Tate Gallery and fine apartments overlooking the river.

But before we go any further, I want to introduce Keith to Billy Fury. Billy, or Ronald William Wycherley as he was known to his mother, was a hero of mine, not least for making it OK to come from Liverpool. The Beatles, a year or two later, went one stage further of course, establishing the city as the cultural centre of the known universe. But Billy paved the way and he is immortalised by a bronze statue at the corner of Albert Dock, looking out across the Mersey where he had worked on a tugboat and as a docker. I am indebted to Peter for the information that Billy is also commemorated by a music stand in Liverpool's Anglican cathedral. Fury died in 1983 at the age of forty-two from heart problems brought on by rheumatic fever but the music lives on. Who can forget his role as Stormy Tempest in the film *That'll be the Day*? Members of his original backing group, the Tornados, still tour the show *Halfway to Paradise* with Colin Gold performing as Billy. I saw it not long ago in Brighton. Rather than knickers being thrown on stage, I suspect from the age of the audience they were incontinence pads.

What I really want to see at Albert Dock is the Merseyside Maritime Museum with its displays on the history of the docks, the *Titanic* (registered in Liverpool), the *Lusitania*, the War in the Atlantic and smuggling. I've been plenty of times before, but I'm interested in revisiting the excellent gallery on slavery. Liverpool infamously built much of its wealth on the proceeds of the transatlantic slave trade, and when I reach Hull I will be visiting the home of the abolitionist William Wilberforce. I'm hoping to find out more here.

As well as the appalling tales of individual suffering involved in the Middle Passage, the exhibition is good on its impact on Africa – the loss of healthy young males from the population, the interruption of pre-existing trade routes and the abandonment of fertile land, all of which set back the development of the continent.

I see that a certain Richard Watt, making his fortune from sugar plantations in Jamaica, brought his wealth back to Merseyside and in 1795 acquired Speke Hall, a fine half-timbered house close to the Mersey, which now finds itself alongside the runway of Liverpool's John Lennon airport. The Hall remained in the Watts family's ownership until 1921 and is now looked after by the National Trust. I plan to be there in two days' time.

The exhibit shows a selection of Liverpool street names, such as Penny Lane made famous by the Beatles, and others named after local businessmen or dignitaries closely linked to slavery and the wealth that it created. One street is named after someone I've been told I'm related to: John Newton, poet and clergyman as well as stalwart of the slave trade, who wrote the words to the Christian hymn, *Amazing Grace*. And, if that doesn't make you ponder…

Leaving the museum, we walk a few hundred yards along the dock road to take in a quick one at the Baltic Fleet pub. Grade I listed, the pub, which now brews on the premises, has a lengthy history of smugglers, press gangs and prostitutes and is very handy for the new youth hostel next door. Moreover, from here we can continue up the hill to the Anglican cathedral. Somehow, we get lost in a housing estate just below – we can see it, but we struggle to reach it – yet when we arrive, I'm astonished. The cathedral is simply massive; no other word will do. Peter, who has sung in the choir there for nearly three decades, has arranged for us to be shown into the organ loft by one of the organists who demonstrates the extraordinary power and range of what was, when completed, the largest musical instrument ever conceived. It continues, with its 10,000 pipes, to be the largest pipe organ in the UK. I forget to ask to see the Billy Fury memorial music stand.

We have a booking for dinner at the Old Blind School and press on towards the restaurant. We are walking through the city's Georgian quarter, an extensive array of beautiful terraced houses. Rodney Street, with its concentration of medical practices, is Liverpool's Harley Street. Falkner Street provided scenes of wartime London for the Foyle's War television series. Hope Street is home to an architectural gem, the glorious Philharmonic Dining Rooms, opposite the Philharmonic Hall, home of the city's top orchestra. Described by no less an authority than CAMRA as "the most spectacular pub in England", the Dining Rooms are a highly ornate treasure with art nouveau metal gates, mosaic floors, wood panelling, rich tiling, leather sofas, stained glass and chandeliers. The pub's most celebrated feature is the gents' urinals, in roseate marble, so we pop in for a quick look round but it's busy in there and I don't fancy taking any photos. It's said that a fledgling pop star from London named Stuart Goddard, while putting these stalls to their proper purpose, caught sight of the brand name Adamant in front of him and was inspired to rename himself Adam Ant...

My destination in Hardman Street was the site of the Liverpool School for the Blind for more than a century from 1851. It has also, at various times, been a police station and a trade union headquarters, and is now an upmarket restaurant. Hearing that I was looking to find places of interest to stay, eat and drink on my walk, a contact recommended the Old Blind School, which she had visited in its guise as the Merseyside Trade Union, Community and Unemployed Resource Centre. I find it a little strange when black pudding is served on a plank and at designer prices, but one must, I suppose, move with the times.

The meal with old friends is heavy with nostalgic, alcohol-fuelled reminiscences, but this was always going to be one of the happy side plots of my Long March.

We talk about the plans for my walk. I mention that volunteering is likely to be a recurring theme and that I've arranged to visit a number of projects along the way which rely heavily on them. I'm employed part-time by one environmental charity and am a volunteer for another; it turns out that my dinner companions are also volunteers in various ways, mainly in connection with local healthcare organisations. We agree that we benefit from this, in terms of keeping mentally or physically active, using any skills that we may have acquired, as well as – we hope – doing something worthwhile for a cause we believe in. Either that or we didn't say "no" quickly and decisively enough when someone asked us.

The four of us wander off in various directions from the restaurant. I am spending two nights at the Adelphi Hotel and wander back down the hill towards the city centre. It has been a long day.

The Adelphi, yet another of the city's listed buildings, served as the most popular place for wealthy passengers to stay in the early 20th century before they embarked on the ocean liners to North America. Guests at the hotel have included F.D. Roosevelt and Winston Churchill and artistes appearing at the Empire Theatre such as Frank Sinatra, Laurel and Hardy, Judy Garland, Bob Dylan, Roy Rogers and his horse Trigger. I am here despite the dire warnings of Peter, who insisted on sharing with me a newspaper article on the Adelphi's award of a zero-food hygiene rating ("urgent improvement necessary") by the city council the previous month. An outbreak of cholera or typhoid will introduce a welcome element of jeopardy to my narrative.

My room smells distinctly smoky, which isn't supposed to happen these days. And, with noisy neighbours in the next room, I turn the bed around, drag it away from the wall and put my faith in 'Muffles Wax Earplugs', without which no trip is complete.

I appear to have survived the night. But then again, I didn't test the output from the kitchens, and last night I spotted a handy McDonald's for breakfast. But first the luxury of an actual bath, which you don't always get in a hotel. When on holiday with my wife, if I wake up first, I'm discouraged from putting the light on in the bedroom and, if there's a bath to hand, I'm inclined to run it and have a long soak and a read to avoid waking her. Over the years I have found it's just not possible to do that in a shower without getting your book soggy.

After breakfast, I wait outside the Adelphi for Peter and Keith. Opposite stands the largely empty shell of the former flagship Lewis's department store. That's not as in John Lewis, but a separate chain operating mainly in the north but also for a while owning Selfridges. The Liverpool store opened the world's first Christmas grotto in 1879 and I can confirm it became a staple of the Liverpool festive season. As I can clearly remember visiting Father Christmas at Lewis's, I can but assume that he switched between here and New Brighton in different years.

I took the opportunity of asking my old friend Lawrence this week whether the expression "don't stand there like one of Lewis's" was confined to my own family. He assured me that the phrase was in common use. It was what your parents said to you if they caught you looking as though you had nothing to do – like one of the mannequins in Lewis's windows.

Liverpool's Lewis's has at least one other claim to fame. Facing me from above the main entrance to the store is a larger than life size statue of a nude man by Jacob Epstein with all his parts in proportion, officially *Liverpool Resurgent* but nicknamed locally 'Nobby Lewis' or 'Dickie Lewis'. It's a popular local meeting place, immortalised in Pete McGovern's song *In My Liverpool Home*: "We speak with an accent exceedingly rare, / Meet under a statue exceedingly bare".

My lift arrives, and I head for a place that one might not expect to find in Liverpool – the National Wildflower Centre, on the edge of the city at the end of the M62 – to meet a former landscape architect colleague of mine from Greater Manchester Council. Margaret has put me in touch with one of its founders, Grant Luscombe. Grant isn't able to meet us on site, but I have arranged to see him at his home in Liverpool later. In the meantime, we have a tour of the centre, which opened in 2001: its aim to encourage the creation of new wildflower habitats for people to enjoy and to provide places where birds, insects and other wildlife can flourish.

The main building demonstrates ecologically sound practices like solar energy, a "green" or living roof and water saving technology while the outside has a composting area and shows how wildflower seeds can be grown and harvested. After our brief tour we head into the visitor centre for elevenses at the Cornflower café. Dave, the volunteer showing us round, tells me that the cowslips make a delicious custard, but I don't know whether he's messing me about. The building seems well used by local families and schools which must be a good thing – so it's sad to learn while writing this book that the centre closed in February 2017.

I visit Grant Luscombe afterwards and we chat in his attractive, low maintenance garden. (My garden in Sussex is also low maintenance but that's just because I don't maintain it.) Grant tells me how, as young graduates from Liverpool University in the 1970s, he and friends pondered where their first gainful employment might come from. As is so frequently the case, an evening in the pub produced answers. They set up a housing co-operative – the second in Liverpool – and a charitable organisation which evolved into Landlife, with the aim of invigorating derelict land through planting native wild flowers. There was no shortage locally of land which would benefit and, with funding from the then Countryside Commission and labour sourced through the government's Job Creation Programme, a start was made on the shores of the Mersey estuary around Speke and the Sankey Canal. The JCP, if I remember correctly from my own work on environmental programmes around Manchester, paid proper union rates and provided meaningful training during the short contract periods – a far cry from today when unemployed but qualified youngsters may be obliged to work at unskilled and inappropriate tasks for no real reward other than to avoid loss of benefits.

Landlife doesn't own or manage land but achieves its aims

by influencing the practices of local authorities and bodies like the Woodland Trust or RSPB. It seeks to inspire youngsters while providing skills training and some of the tools to enter paid employment. Its own income comes from consultancy and, through a trading arm, sales of wildflower seeds. If it is to continue to thrive, it will need to remain small, inventive, flexible and entrepreneurial. It has 120 to 150 members who generally share a philosophy, which will guide the organisation through the changing political and financial environment. This is the kind of project I'm hoping to learn more about during my walk. The demise of the wildflower centre demonstrates some of the practical difficulties but the commitment of those involved remains strong.

My next port of call is another community project based across the road from my holy of holies, Anfield football ground – the home, since 1892, of Liverpool FC and, surprisingly perhaps, for seven years before that, of their old rivals, Everton. I have arranged to meet Britt from Homebaked, and Margaret (whose career took her from landscape architecture to supporting local communities in Liverpool "doing it for themselves"), is keen to see what they have been up to. Anfield residents came together to save their local bakery when, due in part to housing clearance, custom was declining, and the family run business was closing down. The Homebaked Bakery Co-operative was formed, and the bakery reopened in community ownership. Encouraged by this success, Homebaked is tackling – through the Homebaked Community Land Trust – an ambitious scheme of development and regeneration of parts of the local high street, providing workspace for social enterprise, affordable housing and in the words of their website "spaces to meet, chat and celebrate."

We meet Britt at the bakery for lunch. She opts for the scouse pie (it's like scouse, but in a pie) but, with my own lifelong Anfield football connections, I feel duty bound to go for the Shankly pie, named after Liverpool FC's most famous manager. It hits the spot. Britt, who is German but has lived in the area for several years, is a volunteer as a trustee of the charity but is also involved in a paid capacity, working to ensure proper engagement with the local community. While the bakery is fairly quiet during our visit, I know from experience that it is overrun on match days. Britt tells us that the football fans are very supportive and, although Liverpool FC's catering is largely in the hands of one major contractor, Homebaked hope they will soon be supplying scouse pies to the VIP guests.

They have had occasional differences with the city planners about their regeneration proposals but I'm keen to persuade Britt that not all of us planners (did I tell you I was one of those?) are bad people. Homebaked clearly has a healthy network of highly able and committed residents supported by keen and sympathetic "outsiders" in a number of useful professions. It deserves all the success in the world and – this will not be the last time on this walk – I feel inspired by the people I'm meeting. Next time I'm passing, I'll drop off a copy of a satire on town planning for Britt which I hope she will appreciate. I co-wrote it...

Things can only go in a downward direction from here. And they do. I'm to meet up with Keith, Peter and both of his daughters at the art deco George's Dock Building to join a two-hour tour of the Mersey Tunnel.

This is the 1930s Queensway Tunnel linking Liverpool to Birkenhead (the one you saw in Harry Potter and the Deathly Hallows?) rather than the 1971 Kingsway which joins Liverpool to Wallasey further downstream. It's a historic masterpiece and being in some ways over-engineered has stood it in good stead over the years. My father used to say (not all the time, obviously, just every now and again) that he beat a drum at the official opening of the tunnel in 1934. I presume they didn't mind: I think he was in the Boys' Brigade.

The tour is a great £6 worth, taking in the original control room, ventilation stations with their giant fans and the tunnel beneath the tunnel where trams were expected to travel but which now incorporates modern emergency escape refuges. We are told to be on our best behaviour when we pop out into the main tunnel on a short gallery immediately above the rush hour traffic – no hitchhiking gestures, no pretending to speed trap the drivers, no fun at all.

One or two of the tour party are disappointed not to be able to see fish or the Mersey ferry passing overhead, but you can't have everything. I have my own issues throughout the tour: as an inveterate claustrophobe (how on earth did I ever spend all those Saturday afternoons standing with 25,000 others on Anfield's Spion Kop?), I'm not a natural when it comes to confined spaces. See that bit in The Great Escape where they tunnel out under the wire? No way. Anyway, I lurk at the back of the group making sure I know where the exits are.

We emerge from the depths and head to a Lebanese restaurant in Bold Street. From there we have an excellent choice of city centre pubs to tackle; the girls have better things to do this evening but Peter, Keith and I aim for the Roscoe Head because (as if we need an excuse) this historic pub commemorates William Roscoe, Liverpool historian, poet, MP and leading light in the fight for the abolition of slavery, an almost exact contemporary of William Wilberforce. And I don't want the city to be *totally* condemned for its part in that episode of history. Roscoe – also, in his spare time, founder of Liverpool's original botanic gardens and campaigner for free education for the working classes – has been referred to as 'Liverpool's Greatest Citizen' and is commemorated by a street, a garden and, best of all, this pub.

The Roscoe Head is what might be described as a "cracking, old-fashioned little boozer", consisting of a main bar, two small rooms and a tiny snug. It's the only pub in Merseyside and one of only five in the UK to appear in every edition of the CAMRA Good Beer Guide since it was first published in 1974.

It's crowded this evening, but we gather three stools together round the one unoccupied table and start on our "guest beer", Formby IPA. But within seconds we are asked if we've come along for the weekly quiz. We haven't, but it looks as though any normal conversation from us (nostalgic banter and in-jokes) will be irritating to anyone trying to concentrate on the quiz. So, we say yes and work through various rounds of questions which the landlady reads into a microphone from the bar. We dredge up things like: the year that James Dean died; which football team plays at Prenton Park: and what town has a train station called Mumps. In truth we're quite well placed: Keith compiles sports books as a hobby; Peter was once BBC Radio's Brain of Britain; and I'm a dab hand at writing down the answers.

To our natural satisfaction, but also our discomfort, we win. This, we soon discover, means we receive the sum of all of the night's quiz entry fees. They're brought to us in a glass jar and probably amount to £30 to £40. We try to return this, to be added to next week's prize money, but the regulars are having none of this. Eventually a satisfactory agreement is negotiated, and the cash goes to one of the pub's charities, the city's Alder Hey Children's Hospital. We have, in a small way, become honoured guests at the Roscoe Head and new friends arrive from the other rooms to say hello.

We wander out into the night having had a really good time. Peter and Keith head off for a good night's sleep. I walk back to a second night at the Adelphi Hotel.

Chapter 3

Dancing Queens, the Childe of Hale
and a Fine Collection of Truncheons

It's no fault of the Adelphi but I don't have a good night. Ever since I had major heart surgery over ten years ago, the offending organ has the occasional inclination to do its own thing. Syncopation isn't a nice feeling when it's happening to my insides and may require a swift trip to A&E. (I see that Wikipedia gives the definition of *syncopation* as "uneven movement from bar to bar", which is presumably a musical reference but may have been what caused the problem, who knows.)

It's around two in the morning, I'm awake and my heart is all over the place. I know it's too soon to take another of my magic pills: I had one when I turned in and I'm not due another before breakfast. If I take another now it will no doubt sort out the rhythm thing but will also have the effect of leaving me feeling tomorrow that I'm attempting to sleepwalk through treacle – and I have a fair distance to cover.

I don't know what has brought this on. Probably a combination of climbing all those steps up from the Mersey Tunnel tour, which would have tested anyone, plus alcohol and caffeine later in the evening than I'm now used to. There's no way I can get back to sleep so I devote the next few hours to reading and Sudoku, eventually take another pill and manage to doze for an hour or two before facing McDonald's again for breakfast.

A text message arrives from my wife in the early hours asking where the stopcock is. But as my phone is on silent I don't see it until breakfast. Most likely it's no longer a problem. It may have been a joke.

Today will be a proper walking day with Widnes my destination. I'm starting to worry that I may have been too ambitious when planning the journey. I've been inclined over the years to launch out on the occasional lengthy walk without any proper background of regular exercise and it's a long time since I tackled anything like this. And, more or less for the first time, I'm on my own.

I head down towards the river through what was the city's main shopping centre before they opened a big new retail development opposite Albert Dock known as Liverpool One. (Both of the city's top football teams have a merchandising outlet in the new development. Everton's is conspicuously branded as "Everton 2" – which enables it to use as its postal address: "Everton 2, Liverpool 1...") The streets are already busy with shoppers and office workers but there are a few souls asleep in doorways, and the weather looks anything but clement.

Not for the first time, I'm aware of how much the cityscape has changed in Liverpool and other towns and cities since the Clean Air Act. My childhood memories are of blackened, dismal buildings. Now so many of our urban centres are a joy to see. It's hard to rival places like Glasgow, Leeds, Manchester and Liverpool for their wealth of Victorian architecture and a glimpse of the civic pride that encouraged the "city fathers" to build well as testament to their confidence.

I reach the Mersey by the Museum of Liverpool. It's now bitterly cold, the wind is getting up and the river looks extremely rough – I'm surprised to see the ferry putting out from the Pier Head towards Seacombe. This doesn't look like a great way to start the serious business of crossing the country. And rain is now falling steadily. I'm not really one for hats and umbrellas but there is a hood thing attached to my anorak.

I remind myself that, whatever the weather, I need to take notice of my surroundings. With the rain getting heavier, my pocket notebook will be useless, but my wife has told me that my mobile has a facility for recording voice messages, so I have a go. (While writing this account I play back those first recordings. The wind in the background gives it a feel of Scott's last polar jolly, and superimposed on top I hear my barely recognisable self, shouting, "Christ! Why am I doing this??").

I set out from the Adelphi this morning wearing just a short-sleeved t-shirt under my lightweight anorak (this is intended to be basically a summer coast to coast walk) but I have formed the view that I will die unnoticed, here in the centre of one of our largest cities, unless I take measures. I scuttle past the Billy Fury statue – sorry Bill, not interested this morning – into the shelter of the Albert Dock and rummage through my minimalist backpack. As luck, and poor anticipation, would have it, what I need is buried at the bottom, so everything comes out. On top of the t-shirt goes a thermal vest – I wasn't *that* ill-prepared. It feels a little odd that way round but I'm reluctant to strip off the t-shirt too and risk frightening any passing children. On top of the thermal vest goes my one shirt for the week and then the anorak – so, four layers instead of two – and I stagger out again into a sleet-filled gale.

Boy, this is fun.

I shout into my mobile that I'm now passing the legacy sculpture: a gift from the Mormon Church to mark the millions who emigrated from this waterfront in search of a better life – but found America.

Unlike the backside, as it were, of Marine Point in New

Brighton, the river frontage of Albert Dock displays the same quality and attention to detail as the rest of the complex, with a branch of the Tate Gallery and upmarket apartments. There's not so much traffic to see on the river these days but the flats must be very handy for city centre living. It's hard when you're in Liverpool not to be drawn to the Mersey. More than a million people turned out in 2015 to watch Cunard's Three Queens – Queen Mary 2, Queen Victoria and Queen Elizabeth – performing a "river dance", spinning in an orchestrated, stately fashion, to mark the 175th anniversary of Cunard's first transatlantic crossing.

There is no doubt that the city is growing from strength to strength and the experience gained from hosting events and celebrations like European City of Culture has triggered thoughts of hosting the Commonwealth Games in 2026. Both Manchester and Glasgow in recent years have done a magnificent job in that respect. If a bid does go forward from Liverpool, and if it's successful, save me a place for the full duration!

But today I have the river bank more or less to myself. Mad dogs and Englishmen…

And fishermen! I see another lost soul, defying the elements and common sense, setting up for the day. How bad must things be at home…?

With the river, and rain-lashed views of the Wirral shoreline to my right, I trudge past King's Dock – partly infilled but also now home to the Echo Arena, a convention centre and exhibition centre. Another time I must have a proper look around, but this being my first full day's walking, I'm hazy about timings and need to get some steps under my belt. As I work my way along the run of former docks, now being recycled in various ways – to apartments, hotels, a restaurant, and a marina – I'm pleased to see that views remain between the new buildings up to the Anglican cathedral on the skyline. Perhaps this was deliberate.

I may be warmer now in my four layers, but my hands are freezing. (At least Scott had gloves on.) And the rain has changed up a notch from really heavy to ******* *****. I head for a tiny bit of shelter in a doorway and decide to bury my mobile, note book, wallet, map (basically everything from my pockets), deep inside plastic bags in the backpack. For the foreseeable future I'll be relying on my memory.

I press on, occasionally pausing to avoid a wave crashing over the seawall. The last of the docks is the Herculaneum, now partly infilled and surrounded by new housing. I suppose it's necessary and for the better but there seems something incongruent, almost insulting, about the prettified dock when you consider the noise, hard labour and – let's face it – danger of its commercial heyday. Herculaneum was the site of Dingle Station, the southern terminus of the overhead railway, which closed in 1956. Known as the "dockers' umbrella", it connected the docks upstream and down with the Pier Head. The newish Museum of Liverpool at the Pier Head has a brilliant permanent display on its history, including a preserved carriage.

The area known as the Dingle was the setting for Alan Bleasdale's *Boys from the Blackstuff* and Carla Lane's *Bread*, both popular TV series and Liverpool through and through. To borrow again from *In My Liverpool Home*: "We've got places of culture like Dingle and Speke / Where they play "tick" with hatchets, and fight with their feet".

It's just as well that Pete McGovern loved Liverpool… The Dingle also has, or used to have, the "cast iron shore", which conjures up images in the way that, say, the "skeleton coast" does. The name appears to stem either from a local iron foundry, now long gone, or the rust residue after ships were broken up on the foreshore. Perhaps both.

*

Just inland from the river is the home of the Florence Institute, or Florrie, which first opened in 1889 and is surely one of the country's finest historic community buildings. It's a fabulous looking place, built of warm red brick and terracotta with a corner tower and observatory. Financed by a "West Indies merchant" (does that mean what I think it might mean?) and former Lord Mayor of Liverpool, it was built as a memorial to his daughter who had died, aged just 22.

Its aims were to "promote the welfare of" the poor and working boys of the parish and provide them with "a place of instruction and recreation". Probably a step too far to include girls, even in memory of Florence? The institute provided classrooms and a library for bible and other studies and a large gym. It was instantly popular. Boxing became a core activity as thumping each other was clearly an improvement on, er, fighting, and the Florrie also spawned gymnasts and its own football, cricket, baseball and basketball teams. As time went on, it became a hub for nurturing sporting talent from across the city. From my own youth I remember names from boxing like Nigerian-born Dick Tiger and, later, Alan Rudkin.

Music played an important part in the Florrie's appeal. Gerry Marsden learned to play the guitar and held his first skiffle gig here before he became just Gerry.

But after a century of community service, fashions changed, the building showed increasing signs of wear and tear and the Florrie closed. In 1999 a fire destroyed much of the roof and the very real threat of demolition loomed.

The Friends of the Florrie – where would Britain's heritage be without Friends like these – campaigned tirelessly, vigorously hunted down the funds and were rewarded with £3.9 million from the Heritage Lottery towards restoration of the building and returning it to its role as a community centre. This national treasure reopened its doors in 2012. The building now stands almost alone, no longer surrounded by rows of terraced housing, and it's a magnificent sight.

Janine, with whom I've been in prior contact by email, tells me she's originally from Sussex but gained her university qualifications in leisure management and marketing at Liverpool; she's worked in promotion at the Liverpool One shopping development and at the Beatles Story. She introduces me to her chief officer – Anne Lundon, native to the area, with the accent to prove it and with a career in regeneration – who tells me that working at the Florrie and making a contribution to her local community is her dream job, and to Tim, (a member of a band that plays at the Florrie and now working part-time here in customer liaison). They're an infectiously enthusiastic team.

I get my own conducted tour of the building and I see the "before" photographs of it with trees growing through the roof. But it's one thing to secure cash for a major improvement scheme like this and quite another to guarantee a continuing stream of income afterwards to cover the costs of management and maintenance. With this in mind, the Florrie has gained funds from the EU to create new workspace in the building to provide one regular source of income. There are not-for-profit ventures based here, undertaking useful services to the local community; there's a martial arts group, a gym, a library, small meeting rooms, a trust-the-customer snack bar and a very large kitchen. This is now a big venue for receptions and banquets; there's good income from the licensed bar.

The Florrie seems well connected. Ricky Tomlinson brings contacts here to help raise the profile at fundraising events, and Gerry Marsden – without the Pacemakers – helped out with the initial publicity. Former Liverpool FC footballer, John Barnes, is another happy to give his time in the cause.

Janine has invited me to sit in on one of their courses or events to make the most of my visit. I could choose from fitness, family history, local history, guitar, circus skills, Zumba, basic computers and stitch 'n' bitch. I've opted for a session of the History of Liverpool course, and as people start gathering she takes me to the "heritage centre" room with its panels telling the history of the area.

There's a dozen here today, all of us in our 50s or older, and all white, which probably isn't representative of the area nowadays. Lily, who sits down next to me and loves to chat, is eighty-three and has walked here, despite having a bad leg. She feels the institute is once again at the heart of the community – clearly delighted that it's been saved. I'm introduced to the class and everyone seems happy to see me.

The course is not heavyweight material geared towards qualifications, it's a social event where we are all welcome to throw our own knowledge and memories into the pot. We cover a lot of ground very quickly – interesting takes on places and people that we are likely to know. We learn that Jesse Hartley, who built much of Liverpool's most iconic dockland, is related to the Hartleys that make the jam. We talk about the Everyman theatre and how, when it was Hope Hall, it was the first place outside Paris where a film was shown. We hear that we had Britain's first mosque, in 1887, and the first purpose built cinema, the Futurist – sadly now on the point of being demolished. I'm up for this – I tell them that I took a very pretty girl to see Doctor Zhivago at the Futurist back in the 1960s. The chap opposite tells me that I wasn't the only one, but I think he's talking about a different girl. I chip in with memories of travelling on the old overhead railway along the docks and my own experience of the religious divisions in the city.

Phil knows his audience. "I'm going to be controversial now," he says. We sit and wonder what's coming. "Not all Tories are bad."

This concept looks unlikely to gain traction, but we'll give it a go – we're in a generous mood. It turns out Phil is talking about Michael Heseltine who gave us our International Garden Festival and a reopened Albert Dock.

I'm having a really good time and I'm sorry when the session comes to an end. My new student friends want to hear about my walk, and whether I'll be back next week. It's tempting.

The rain is easing as I reach the start of Otterspool Promenade. The area was used to dispose of household waste and excavated material from the older Mersey tunnel and, after reclamation and landscaping, opened in 1950 as parkland. In 1984 the promenade became the site for Britain's first International Garden Festival. I remember it well as the festival turned out to be the last thing I took my mother to before she died that year. The handful of garden festivals which took place around the country were a symbol of the efforts of Michael Heseltine, the former Tory minister, held in greater affection in Liverpool than is normal for someone of his political party. In the face of opposition from some of his cabinet colleagues, Heseltine, sent to the city in the wake of the Toxteth riots, argued for resources to be devoted to regeneration measures. Heseltine received the Freedom of Liverpool – from a Labour council – in 2012.

The sky is brightening at last, and I'm due to meet Edward, a landscape architect and colleague from my days at Greater Manchester Council, just this side of the Garston docks. Edward has offered to show me work that he and his practice have been working on: a stretch of coastal grassland and wetland between the river on one side and the National Trust property of Speke Hall on the other. The Peel Group, a company with major ownerships and property developments around Manchester, Liverpool and Birkenhead, have contracted Edward to improve the wildlife habitat and landscape along the coastal strip and establish continuous footpath access. The views across the Mersey from the Garston and Speke Coastal Reserve are worth the effort and a completed coastal walk will be a great asset.

Edward drives us to the nearest village, Hale; a quiet, attractive backwater separated from the car factories and housing estates of Speke and Halewood by just a few fields. We go for a pub lunch at the Childe of Hale, named after John Middleton whose gravestone in the local churchyard carries the epitaph, "Here lyeth the bodie of John Middleton the Childe of Hale. Nine feet three. Born 1578 Dyed 1623."

The pub's sign bears a copy of a portrait of John Middleton that resides in Brasenose College in Oxford. Across the road from the church is a three-metre-tall – or life size, if you will – bronze statue of the village's most famous resident.

It is said that the Childe slept at night with his feet hanging out of the window of his small house. He served as bodyguard to the Sheriff of Lancashire – I mean, you're not going to pick a fight with that, are you – and was presented in court to King James I.

After lunch, Edward drives me along a quiet lane to a point from where we are able to walk to Hale lighthouse for a further view of the river. He tells me this is the most southerly point of the old county of Lancashire. As I once spent time searching for the most easterly point of the British mainland (it's near Lowestoft, it's a gentle curve in the promenade and that's two hours I'll never get back), I'm up for this. The only people we see parked along the road appear to be spotting planes landing and taking off at John Lennon Airport, fly tipping or socialising enthusiastically in cars.

Then, with some regret on my part, Edward drops me off, so I can resume my walk to Widnes.

The words "duck decoy" are marked a few hundred yards away on my map and that should lead to a brief detour and a fascinating paragraph or two on the history and design of these historic trapping devices. But I'm knackered, I'm not going off route and you can read about them yourselves. I press on.

I cross Pickerings Pasture, a wildflower meadow established on an old landfill site – perhaps Landlife has been busy here. And then in late afternoon I reach the outskirts of Widnes. There is a large Tesco warehouse and something like a hundred Eddie Stobarts lined up alongside. Shouldn't I be identifying butterflies, birds and plant species, not getting exercised about HGVs?

This is the widest part of the Mersey. It seems to be flowing downstream nearest to the shore but upstream – presumably on an incoming tide – further out. That's geography for you. There are breakers where the two streams are in conflict, despite there now being no wind. Diving birds are gathered in this conflict zone and there are hundreds of waders on the extensive mudflats.

I contend with one unhelpful descent and ascent to cross a small ravine, make it to Widnes at the end of my first full day's walking and check into the Mersey Hotel. This is notable for an unrivalled view (or it would be if it hadn't started pouring again) of the viaduct which soars high above the pub carrying the A533 over the Mersey and the Manchester Ship Canal. You wouldn't call the structure pretty but it's uncompromising and undoubtedly impressive in scale.

The surroundings may be a tad industrial, but the hotel is a friendly place. My room is spotless with a very welcome bath and the largest TV screen I've ever seen outside a sports bar. It has all I need – I'm not really looking for excitement this evening so much as an alcohol-induced coma – except for food served in the evening, which its website had promised me. Which means out into the rain again and a tired trudge uphill – strangely, it proves to be uphill in both directions – to a different pub where I dine on a £5 "Chinese curry with rice and chips", as you do. The locals are watching Manchester City play Paris Saint-Germain on Sky Sports and are clearly cheering for PSG, which suggests that I'm still closer to Liverpool than Manchester.

Thursday's walk begins along Widnes's pleasant Victoria Promenade, the kind of feature you might expect at the seaside rather than in an industrial town facing another industrial town, Runcorn, across an industrial river. Victorian Widnesians would stroll here of an evening and enjoy the distant views of the Welsh hills. Only if, I assume, they were visible through the industrial smog.

There is a tradition that the song *Homeward Bound* was written by Paul Simon at Widnes station. There is a quote allegedly from Simon as follows: "If you know Widnes, then you'll understand how I was desperately trying to get back to London as quickly as possible." Which is harsh. Obviously, he hadn't been here for the rugby league.

I cross the lock where the Sankey Canal enters the Mersey onto Spike Island. This was the heart of the town's thriving chemical industry from the middle of the 19th century, exploiting its rail and canal links and abundant water supply but also giving rise to exceptional levels of pollution even by Victorian standards. The Island – reclaimed marshland separated from the mainland by the canal – is now an attractive mix of parkland and woodland and a setting for the Catalyst Science Discovery Centre, the only museum in the UK devoted solely to chemistry. I'm tempted but I already have an arrangement to meet old colleagues at another museum later in the day and there's only so many museums you can be expected to handle.

I pass an interpretive panel about the area's industrial history with maps, artists' impressions and helpful descriptive text. It carries the description of Widnes as "the dirtiest, ugliest and most depressing town in England" *(1888: Daily News)* and "a poisonous hell-town" *(1905: Daily Mail)*. And, no doubt to bring the picture up to date, "The site is now occupied by a Brewers Fayre."

Perhaps I do Paul Simon an injustice.

I reach the end of Spike Island and meet a sign that tells me that the path I'm following – part of the Trans Pennine Trail at this point – has been temporarily closed during the construction of the Mersey Gateway (a six-lane toll bridge linking Widnes and Runcorn across the Mersey and the Ship Canal). Rather than await the reopening of the path, I retrace my steps and follow the totally rubbish diversion signs through the town. I know I'm here to enjoy the walking but I'm not looking for any extras.

Leaving Widnes, I'm following the bank of the Sankey or St. Helens Canal to Warrington. To my left it's an uncompromisingly industrial and commercial landscape of factories, trading estates and dereliction; to my right the broad sweep of the Mersey, its marshes and mudflats. I can see the cooling towers of Fiddler's Ferry power station in the distance which is encouraging. But they remain in the distance for a depressingly long time.

I pass a sign bearing the legend "Warrington in the Heart of the Mersey Forest", which is pushing it a bit. It also reads *Hull 161 miles Hornsea 177 miles* and I'm pleased it isn't in kilometres because I can't handle large numbers today.

I've been able to see the cooling towers for an hour now and they're still the same size.

I try looking the other way, think of something else, play with my mobile. They're still the same size.

Two young girls on bikes approach from the Warrington

direction and ask me how to get to the power station, which is still ahead of me on the other side of the canal. Other than them turning around and cycling back to Warrington or carrying on all the way to Widnes and back on the far side of the canal, I have no idea, but they are the first humans I've encountered for days and this has to be an encouraging sign. OK, it may not have been as long as that, but it's been a long morning.

I arrive almost by accident at an extremely welcome sight: The Ferry Tavern pub between the canal bank and the northern bank of the Mersey. It's not due to open for another ten minutes but I'm in no mood to pass by without a pint of something wet. I fear that if I sit down while waiting for it to open, I may not get up again, so I opt for leaning entreatingly on the door until the barman responds. It's good to be refreshed but it's a b*gg*r to get going again afterwards.

I eventually reach Warrington and arrive, as one does on a canal, via its armpit. Enticingly located at the entrance to a sewage works and household waste site is Linda's burger van. I'm not very hungry, having started the day with a fry up at the Mersey Hotel in Widnes, but there's a hand-written sign reading *Red Hot Spam on Toast £1.30* and I was never going to pass up on that. Not when there's free use of a towel to wipe down the wet chair and unlimited ketchup.

It turns out that Linda was brought up in Everton Valley, just a longish throw-in from Anfield. She expresses interest in my walk but says her own preference is for the Lake District, which is fair enough. Linda hopes to retire to live in the sun and I hope she makes it. Her Hot Spam is excellent.

Heading into the town centre of Warrington, I spot Food-4Thought which offers "2 Bacon two Sausages and Egg for £3", which seems unbeatable, except that I've just overloaded on Red Hot Spam. There are limits, even for me.

I pass Dunky's Day Nursery in what looks from the outside to be a clapped out old pub behind the war memorial. I hope it looks better inside. Signs lead me to the Cultural Quarter. I've arranged to meet Wendy and Mac, both colleagues from my time with Greater Manchester Council. I've booked a conducted tour for the three of us at the Museum of Policing in Cheshire. Because I know how to have a good time.

The museum is run by volunteers with support in the form of premises, artefacts and so on provided by the Cheshire Constabulary. Until quite recently the building was a working police station, the headquarters of the Warrington Division, but the police have more or less moved out now and it seems likely that the museum will have to relocate. Volunteers Peter and Mary Quinn are expecting us and have put on the kettle.

I've been expecting: "truncheons through the ages"; displays on the rich heritage of kettling; how to fit up known villains with "evidence"; and the casualty rates associated with high speed car chases. It's not to be, but we have a great time being shown round an informative and professionally presented exhibition by two enthusiastic and highly knowledgeable volunteers. There are murder weapons, films and photos, newspaper crime reports, actual cells, police sports trophies (very good at tug of war, apparently) – and, OK, a collection of truncheons through the ages. We seize the opportunity to dress up in high vis jackets like Sarah Lancashire in *Happy Valley* and pose aggressively for group photos in full armed response gear. Magic. On my way out, I buy a CD of the Band of the Cheshire Constabulary *In Concert* – and really enjoy it when I'm home, though my wife insists it stays in the car, for my personal use only.

From the museum to the Best Western hotel nearby where I'm booked in for tonight. I've generally favoured staying at places along the route with some history, or architectural interest, or quirk, but sometimes it's a case of "what is there that's close to my route?" I'm in a ground floor room and there's a wedding party occupying much of the hotel. It's turned out quite warm and many of the guests remain in the courtyard into the early hours – right outside my window. I feel very curmudgeonly and hope it rains on the wedding. The wax earplugs come in useful again.

When I switch on my mobile in the morning there's a text message from my wife asking where her train ticket is as she's coming up tomorrow. And one from our daughter saying she's run out of money and it's only the 8th of the month. And my big toes are sore from rubbing against my new walking shoes. I'm not sure that counts as "jeopardy" for the purposes of dramatic travel writing but it hurts.

Another blowout breakfast. Probably not a great idea. But it's included in the price, so I feel obliged to do it justice. I tell myself it's a post-war generation thing.

From the hotel, my route takes me first alongside the Ship Canal, then I pick up the Trans Pennine Trail which consists here of a long stretch of former railway, the old Warrington to Altrincham line. Generally, this makes for pleasant, easy walking except where the whole trackbed has been flooded by recent rain and my new lightweight footwear isn't fit for purpose.

Along the trail they've constructed what I believe are called squeeze stiles, aimed at blocking motor bikes but permitting access for walkers, and cyclists provided they dismount. They're in the form of two metal frames which converge towards the top. Fine. But if you stand more than five foot six tall and you're carrying a backpack, you're obliged either to take it off and carry it past the constriction or lower yourself with back straight and your sack *in situ* in a kind of limbo motion. Now, most of my moving parts have seen better days: admittedly there's a left knee that has only ten years on the clock and a right hip that's less than three years old, but there are some distinctly dodgy elements upstream and downstream. Last time I had knees that coped well with that kind of manoeuvre, kipper ties were in fashion and we still had a welfare state.

And then I suffer my first equipment malfunction. At Thelwall, of M6 viaduct fame, where my old railway line runs just a few yards from the towpath of the Bridgewater Canal, a strap on my backpack gives way and I mumble "oh, no", or words to that effect. Obviously not intended for carrying things, the stitching hasn't coped and one of the straps is no longer attached at both ends. I find it hard to envisage cuddling the pack in my arms for the rest of the day but impress myself by carrying out a sort of repair which I hope may see me through.

I reach what was once Lymm station, which has an information board about the line and how much Doctor Beeching contributed to the building of the nation's cycle network. There are nice photos and maps of the former Lymm Hotel by the station, with a fine ballroom and horse-drawn taxis.

Today's route isn't taking me past much in the way of shop or pub, but I do come across a small Co-op supermarket just before what was once Heatley station. I eat a healthy lunch of orange juice and Quavers perched uncomfortably on a bollard outside. I think this only constitutes one of my five daily portions of fruit and veg. Perhaps cheese and onion crisps would have given me another one.

I have a fair bit of walking to do this afternoon through the Cheshire countryside, but I will get a break after today. Soon I reach a point where the old railway line crosses the River Bollin, which here forms the boundary between the boroughs of Warrington and Trafford, and indeed between Cheshire (as defined since 1974 anyway) and Greater Manchester.

Near Dunham station, as was, a bronze plaque set in a stone at the side of the track bears a map and proclaims the achievement of the Bollin Valley Partnership 1973 to 2013, "Forty Years of Countryside Management". Now this means something to me. From 1973 to 1986 I was one of the local authority staff responsible for this work.

The Countryside Commission, a government quango, set up a small number of experimental projects aimed at sorting out land management issues and conflicts. The Bollin Valley was selected for a project on the "urban fringe" where farmers operated in a climate of uncertainty over the prospects of development, pressures for public access and occasional trespass and vandalism. Half of the valley was in the shiny new county of Greater Manchester, with whom I began my first proper job.

The work on the ground was mainly in the hands of a small number of khaki-clad rangers who aimed to keep the farming community sweet by helping to rebuild broken down fences, gates and stiles, while persuading them to stop shooting at members of the public. But, as their contribution, local councils and other statutory bodies pretended to work together on planning, highways and other more formal stuff. I don't know if we helped that much, but we could have got in the way if we had set our minds to it.

I wonder if, in the thirty years that have passed since then, that footpath diversion I was working on has gone ahead...

The landscape to either side of my route – give or take the odd line of pylons – looks in good heart, all green fields and well maintained red brick buildings. The day has remained dry, but the temperature has varied, and I keep stopping to add or take off a layer. The emergency repair work on the backpack seems to be holding but I'm supporting the weight awkwardly with one hand.

On the outskirts of Altrincham – effectively the south west corner of the Manchester conurbation – I swap my Trans Pennine Trail route along the railway line for the towpath of the Bridgewater Canal where the two routes run close. It's shorter, and this matters.

The towpath is well surfaced, we're arriving in a built-up area and it's late Friday afternoon. I've more or less had the day to myself until now but I'm starting to see walkers, cyclists, joggers, even picnickers. And the accents I'm hearing are no longer from Merseyside.

My energy levels are well down and I'm glad I don't have to keep up with anybody or talk to them. Perhaps a cooked breakfast and Quavers isn't ideal. I may not have much further to go this afternoon but I'm in need of a rest. I find an awkwardly sloping stone plinth to park my rear on while I get out my copy of Friday's *Guardian* and tackle the Sudoku. Does that sound weird? Friday's is one of the difficult Sudokus – they get harder as the week goes by – and I hope my morale won't be irrevocably damaged if I can't hack it.

I'm now in phone contact with Mac. In the past I've enjoyed many walking holidays with him in this country and abroad, though on reflection I'm not sure that either of us much liked the actual walking part. Mac lives nearby and has promised to look out for me and stop me falling into the canal when I'm at a low ebb. I think he's somewhere further along the canal in Sale.

I make to get up from my sloping seat but slide alarmingly and embarrassingly sideways and on to the ground. Had there been anyone nearby they would have felt obliged to rush to the rescue of the poor old chap now lying on his back by the canal, having no doubt ensured that I'd "gone viral" first. This is truly awful. There's nothing damaged other than my self-esteem but that's bad enough and I flounder about in a desperate effort to get upright before anyone comes along.

Half an hour later I reach Mac on the towpath by Sale station and he does what comes most naturally to him. He leads me to his local pub which is close by and gets two rounds in. Mac is another one who volunteers, in his case for a cancer charity, but I notice that he doesn't volunteer to carry my backpack.

From the pub I am grateful to be collected by Helen, a former flatmate from my Manchester days and close friend for over forty years, and driven to her house in Marple for the night. She feeds me healthily, involving stuff like fruit and vegetables, and I'm in no position to complain. Her husband Phil, who is a doctor, looks at my blackened toenails, and tuts. While Helen talks in a vain attempt to distract me, and I bite down on a sock, Phil clips the offending nails and bursts a blister beneath one of them. I apologise as quantities of pus leak out onto the floor. Phil tells me it's actually called exudate, but it's still not nice.

I notice that my repair job on the strap of the backpack is quite literally hanging by a single thread. Thankfully today is my last walking day for a few weeks, and I resolve to ditch the bag. I found it in the loft at home and have no idea where it came from. I feel no attachment: I suspect it belonged to an old swain of my daughter's who was presumably also ditched at some stage, and who may for all I know also be in the loft. I decide to send the new walking shoes to a deserving cause. I would welcome some new feet but that's something to think about another day.

It's Saturday and my wife is heading up on the train from Sussex as we have a sociable weekend planned. But first I'm due over for morning coffee with friends and former colleagues who live handily near to where I'm staying in Marple.

David Sumner has long been a canal nut and spent more time than seemed feasible on efforts to restore the Huddersfield Narrow Canal which ran for nearly twenty miles, connecting Ashton on the east side of Manchester with Huddersfield. It had closed in 1944 and had fallen into disrepair. He was also responsible for persuading me to take my only proper trip on a canal boat. David needed some hands to help him to deliver a narrow boat from Keighley in Yorkshire to an event somewhere in the Midlands, but I'm convinced he also had in mind exposing one or two of us colleagues to the merits of a functioning canal network. Anyway, he was supplying beer money and bacon butties and I wasn't arguing.

On the day in 1986 when Margaret Thatcher abolished Greater Manchester Council along with Greater London Council and the other metropolitan county councils, the Labour-controlled GMC made a number of deathbed grants to causes they had been supporting and wished to see succeed after their own demise. David's Huddersfield Canal Society, formed twelve years earlier, received £1.8 million in the days when that would still have bought you a top football team rather than covered a full back's champagne bill for a week. The Society's bank manager, used to dealing with the members' subs and coffee fund, had to be resuscitated.

In the years since, with a huge voluntary effort and funds from various sources, the canal has been totally restored and fully reopened in May 2001. My walk will eventually take me alongside the canal and over and through the Pennines – I say "through" as the highest and longest tunnel on Britain's canal network, the Standedge, lies in wait. David lends me a handful of books and maps of the canal to furnish me with background reading and something heavy to carry. Now the president of the canal society, he received an MBE for his services to canal restoration, and very well deserved.

I pick up a hire car and collect my wife from Stockport station. With our hosts Helen and Phil, we meet up in Manchester's Chinatown on Saturday evening with John and Maggie, our friends and neighbours from Sussex, whose son James is competing in the local marathon. The next day we are all on the streets to show our support. James spots us in the crowd but is not inclined to stop for a chat – he finishes in under two and a half hours and his running club from Brighton wins the team prize.

I have taken part in this marathon twice myself in the distant past. I would say I was a "fun runner" but I don't remember it feeling like fun when I was doing it. My own perspective is that I cut quite a rugged figure with my then trendy towelling headband and wrist bands and my shock of thick black hair, but this image was dented recently when I showed a photograph that I was particularly fond of to a language class and it produced a spontaneous cry of "118 118!"

I recall an unpleasant incident during one of these events. While running through Old Trafford, liquid began to trickle down my leg. This was both scary and embarrassing. I remembered something in Bruce Tulloh's book about jogging, which referred to possible irreparable damage one might incur to one's innards from excessive running. Stopping seemed a sensible option but I knew there would be a problem with restarting. Tentatively, as I ran, I touched the inside of my leg with a finger and even more tentatively I put my finger to my lips. Nothing obvious. I kept going, my mind churning.

Five minutes later there was a flash of recall – I remembered grabbing a wet sponge from someone on the pavement a few miles back, stuffing it down the back of my running vest and forgetting about it. Oh, thank you, Lord! Thank you!

After James's marathon, my wife and I head off to Dunham

Massey, a National Trust property nearby, and then to Anfield where we have tickets for Liverpool's match against Stoke. The team is "in transition" which is where we've been since around 1992. With the state of the club at present, the enjoyment usually peaks not during the game itself but five minutes before kick off with a full-throated rendering of *You'll Never Walk Alone*, which has me on Strepsils for the remainder of the week.

I have to go back to work for a few weeks and must resume my journey later. Before travelling home to Sussex, however, I have another appointment back in Liverpool. Hull, where I'm heading on my walk, has been designated UK City of Culture for 2017, and I want to find out what being European Capital of Culture in 2008 meant to Liverpool. I've been put in touch with Leah Abbott who works at Liverpool's Everyman Theatre. Leah was away on holiday while I was wandering the sights of the city a week ago but is back and has kindly offered to give me a personal tour. The theatre has recently been remodelled and the changes have been attracting positive noises from architectural critics and punters alike.

Sometimes called Liverpool's third cathedral, the Everyman sits on Hope Street, the road which links the other two. Formerly a chapel, the building has also served as a cinema, night club and coffee bar and in 1964 became the base for a new, adventurous theatre to complement the more traditional theatres like the Playhouse. Directors like Terry Hands and Ken Campbell, actors and performers like Barbara Dickson, Julie Walters, Antony Sher, Jonathan Pryce, Pete Postlethwaite, Bill Nighy, Alison Steadman, David Morrissey have all made their mark at the Everyman – and it has doubtless made its mark on them and their careers.

Leah shows me just about everything: front of stage; backstage; the make-up and costume departments; quiet resting spaces for actors; the room provided for local people free of charge, so they can write (away from the distractions of home), which is a simple but nice touch.

She is in no doubt that the heightened confidence, profile and experience that came with the Capital of Culture tag have contributed to the city's willingness to take things on. There had previously been cynicism from visitors and outsiders content to run with tired old Liverpudlian stereotypes but local people, according to Leah, would regard its year as Capital of Culture as highly successful with a continuing legacy of artistic enterprise. Hull may be starting from an even more humble base, and I feel I can already hear the negative noises, but the arts and culture, however defined, are increasingly at the heart of successful regeneration schemes like the Turner Contemporary gallery in Margate and the Jerwood in Hastings. I'm looking forward to Hull and now I think I have a clearer idea of the questions that I want to put.

And when our tour and our chat have finished, Leah sets off to discharge another of her responsibilities at the Everyman, at a meeting of the theatre's beekeeping group – which is just as it should be.

Mrs A has been pottering around the city centre while I've been at the Everyman, and is happy for us to tarry a while longer. We're close to the Roman Catholic Metropolitan Cathedral and I haven't set foot in there for over forty years. Now I don't claim detailed knowledge of cathedral architecture and I have had no religious belief since my fervent childhood prayers about Elizabeth Shufflebotham and being picked to play for Liverpool FC went sadly unanswered, but the interior of "Paddy's Wigwam" is (if one may borrow a word overused in connection with Premiership centre halves), awesome. Light, colourful and airy – just gorgeous.

Nearby is a sad-looking building that is familiar from a recent BBC documentary. The Wellington Rooms, built in 1815/16 in neo-classical style and used by high society for dance balls and parties, and more recently as a centre for the city's Irish community, has fallen on hard times and has been unoccupied for twenty years. If ever a quality building needed and deserved a better future, this is a good candidate. I hope it finds someone able to embrace it with love and affection. They say it served excellent Guinness.

On the spur of the moment, we decide to see "the Gormleys" while we're here. My wife says this is the first time that she has "really got" Liverpool and I don't want to stand in her way. We drive out to Crosby to see Antony Gormley's *Another Place*, a hundred cast-iron life-size figures spread along two miles of the foreshore and stretching half a mile out to sea. They are made from casts of the artist's body and stand on the beach looking vacant (like one of Lewis's?)

According to Gormley, "Here…the prevalence of sky seems to question the earth's substance…human life is tested against planetary time…just the industrially reproduced body of a middle-aged man trying to remain standing and trying to breathe".

We agree it looks nice. We also agree that it's getting late for driving to Sussex today and decide to stay overnight in the extraordinary Titanic Hotel in Stanley Dock. Remember that bit at the start, where I mentioned it was OK for me to go travelling on my own as long as Mrs A felt she wasn't missing out on anything expensive? Well, now that she's here…

This conversion of a massive former rum warehouse lies some way north of Albert Dock and the buzz of the city centre, a bold step in regenerating the northern dockland. Stanley Dock is where the Liverpool Leeds Canal reaches the Mersey, or it was until 2009 when a new link was constructed connecting a number of docks and paralleling the Mersey to enable canal boats to reach the Pier Head and beyond.

The Titanic Hotel's bedrooms, extending the width of the warehouse with a very broad central corridor complete with original loadbearing iron columns, are themselves enormous – by far the largest hotel bedrooms I have ever stayed in. If nature should happen to call in the night, I hope there is plenty of warning.

Being some way from the city lights means we are more or less committed to spending the evening here. I tackle the huge plasma screen in the room: my options on the home page menu include "the big adventure" (I can't remember; probably things to do), "the big sleep" (tells you about the pillows), "the knowledge" (emergency numbers, I think) and "it's about all of us" (our staff are nice and try hard). The coffee machine is highly sophisticated but there are no instructions and I can't work it. There is also a traditional tea and coffee making arrangement involving a kettle, which I'm good at. But no mugs or stirrers, so I use a couple of glasses from the bathroom and wrap a sock round them as they're hot. Afterwards I find all the stuff in a cupboard right next to the kettle.

Dinner is elegant, and tastefully presented, which means I'm hungry afterwards and ask at the bar for salted peanuts or scratchings. Not being a proper pub, they can't produce these, but a waiter offers to fetch me something from the staff vending machine. Which is why I love Liverpool.

Chapter 4

Ghost Riders in Stalybridge

I've been blogging about my walk, in order to attract sponsorship contributions for my chosen charity and this has been picked up by a student journalist at university back home in Sussex. He asks if he can interview me for a piece which he thinks he can get into the local paper and we arrange to meet. On the same morning, I have fixed an appointment with a chiropodist to see what can be done about my big black, walk-battered toenails (readers of a sensitive disposition may wish to look away now). He opts for toenailectomy, which is a new look for me, and afterwards I walk gingerly across the road to a café to meet my student.

He asks why I'm doing the walk, how far I'm hoping to do each day, how it's gone so far, what's still to come. It's great to share my thoughts and experiences with someone who's interested. I throw in plenty of anecdotes and mention where I've been immediately before our meeting.

I pick up a copy of the *Sussex Express* later in the week to see if I'm in there. There's a big article with a photo under a bold headline: *66 Year Old Chiropodist Patient Plans East to West Trek.*

It's the end of April and I'm back for the second week of my walk, which will involve around 35 miles of walking and take me from one side of Greater Manchester to the other. In Liverpool, I wanted to take in as much as possible of my native city as my visits over the years have tended to be brief. In Manchester, where I worked for 20 years, I'm already familiar with most of the obvious attractions. I plan to revisit one or two favourites and dig a little deeper into some of the places and projects which have a rather lower public profile. And there will be old friends and colleagues in and around Manchester happy to update me.

I need to pick up the walk from where I finished earlier in the month, in Sale on the towpath of the Bridgewater Canal, but that can wait until tomorrow. First, I have business in the city centre and from the train I head for the office of the Manchester Modernist Society.

I'm not an architect but a town planner by former profession. Without understanding every detail of what I'm looking at, I do appreciate decent old buildings. I may not be able to tell my architrave from my spandrel, but I can spot a bit of quality when I see it, and feel better for it. We lose so much of what we value in our landscapes and townscapes simply because someone can make more money by grubbing something up or knocking something down but, happily, there are people around who are prepared to poke their noses in and press for better solutions. My journey this year will take me to some revered old buildings, down on their luck but hoping for a brighter future, and I believe I'm about to meet some people who value 1960s and 70s concrete. I'm not sure there will be a national love-in for all things Brutalist, but the National Trust has been organising walks and talks on London's South Bank and some of the finer examples of the genre are being protected through the listing procedure. One 1960 building which never lacked for fans, including me, stands close to where I lived at one time on the south side of Manchester.

The seven-storey building has been known forever as the Toast Rack because its parabolic concrete exterior frame looks like one, though much bigger obviously and without a visible crumb tray. And with a low-rise, round building at its foot ("the poached egg"), the Hollings Building was built for the Domestic Trades College, which seems entirely appropriate. Having become in its turn part of Manchester Poly and then the city's Metropolitan University, the Toast Rack was described by architectural critic Nikolaus Pevsner as "a perfect piece of pop architecture" and Grade II listed by English Heritage. The campus closed in 2013 and the Toast Rack awaits a new future as private rented flats.

The Modernist Society put in a stint as "creatives in residence" at the Toast Rack during its final academic year "to act as a catalyst and instigators for a programme of collaborations and explorations involving a variety of artists, writers, researchers, students, staff and other members of the Hollings Faculty community." Highlights of this collaboration included: a visit from the building's now 83-year-old architect (formerly of the City Architect's Department); the brewing of Toast Rack ale; and the finding of a trophy awarded to the building by the Australian Egg Board.

I have prepared for my visit by buying and skimming through a brand-new publication, *Raw Concrete: the Beauty of Brutalism* and I can tell already that any bibliography for this book will be eclectic.

Barnabas Calder, author of *Raw Concrete*, doesn't hold back:

> Brutalism was the high point of architecture in the entire history of humanity. It takes only a fairly basic level of expertise to start to recognise it as one of the greatest ever flowerings of human creativity and ingenuity.

Calder's selected case studies don't unfortunately include any examples from Manchester, but his passions ring out. He hymns the praises of the National Theatre, recognised by an official Historic England listing, but deplores the lack of equivalent status for the Southbank Centre nearby, with its Hayward Gallery and concert halls.

He describes his salvaging of a chunk of concrete from a partial demolition of Paisley's Brutalist Civic Centre in 2010. When moving house from Glasgow, he told the movers it was a fragile ornament, hoping they might mistake it for a sculpture or a fossil and treat it with appropriate care. The man who packed it wrapped it well, but his label on the box was clear enough: 'lump o' concrete'. When it was explained what it was, he crossed out his label and wrote instead: 'precious relic of car park'.

Jack Hale and Eddy Rhead, whom I'm meeting at the Modernist Society office, explain that they are not architects, not focused specifically on concrete and nor are they essentially a campaigning body. There are other organisations like the Twentieth Century Society who take up the cudgels on behalf of good modern buildings under threat; the Modernist Society sees itself as celebrating the best of post WW1 constructions, whether red phone boxes or flyovers, through urban rambles, music, talks, picnics or film screenings, all promoted via social media. They have writer and film-maker Jonathan Meades and Johnny Marr of The Smiths as patrons and a wide Facebook group (rather than a subs-paying membership), with some limited income to cover office costs from sales of T-shirts, mugs and other merchandise, as well as a quarterly magazine and payments received for projects. There are no staff.

We discover that all three of us have bought and enjoyed the 2015 coffee table book, *Soviet Bus Stops*, but I'm not sure if this is entirely a good thing.

After our meeting I read through a copy of their magazine, *The Modernist*, and there's an article devoted to the Goblin Teasmade.

Tonight, I'm booked into Castlefield Youth Hostel on the edge of the city centre. There are more than enough hotels in the city of course but I thought the hostel would make a change. I don't want it to be too much of a change – I know they won't be putting the lights off at 10 o'clock (though I guess that would be fine) and I won't have to sweep the floor or retile the roof before I get my card back in the morning. I'm not up for sharing a dormitory so I've booked a room for four at a cost of £50 and I'm keeping it for myself. I'm banking on my own snoring not keeping me awake.

Castlefield – once a thriving area of warehousing activity around the junction of the Rivers Irwell and Medlock and the Bridgewater, Rochdale and the Mersey and Irwell Navigation Canals – deteriorated in the middle of the 20th century into an extensive area of dereliction and urban decay. But, as an example of what can be done to bring such places back from the dead, it would be hard to find a better one. Happily, enough of the fine industrial heritage survived to form the basis for major renewal from the 1980s and 90s and the waterways are now lined with upmarket apartments, bars, restaurants and my bedroom for the night. The hostel is a bright, smart, modern building in a splendid location alongside the canal.

There's enough rain falling this afternoon and evening in Castlefield to fill a dozen canal basins, but the hostel serves to dry me out before I head off again to meet Anne, an ex-colleague, for dinner at *Albert's Shed*, where I know that dozens of my former GMC workmates still meet regularly for lunch to complain about Margaret Thatcher. It's still raining hours later when I walk with Anne back to her train, and then return to the hostel along some distinctly deserted towpaths.

The foyer seems to be the best place to get a wi-fi connection and I'm soon joined by Sonia, a young lady up from Lewisham for an interview for a place on a drama course. She presumably regards me as a marginal improvement on solitude and confirms my assumption that staying at the hostel is likely to be more sociable than the Premier Inn. This turns out to be Sonia's first visit to Manchester – she's here for a few days – and asks my advice on places to see. I give that my best shot, but her number one priority is the Trafford Centre (like a giant shopping mall, only uglier), so we're not really on the same wavelength. She heads off to her room with a friendly, "Probably see you at breakfast!"

I wake in one of my four bunk beds to yet more heavy rain, and to add insult to injury, I encounter a difficulty with my en-suite shower.

I'm travelling light because everything has to be carried on my back, so no soap, no shampoo, no towels, and I'm relying on some all-purpose stuff that emerges from a fitting on the shower wall. My wife has warned me that the lack of a proper shampoo and conditioner will mean I'll end up with "residues" in my hair, and I understand this to be very bad. "There's nothing worse." But I say that you just have to live life on the edge sometimes.

My real shower-based problem stems from the fact that when you switch on the water, the hose thing spins round and shoots its contents out of the cubicle and into the room. It clearly needs to be gripped but I need a hand to reach for the gel stuff and another to close the door. This seems intractable and would, I'm certain, test the coping strategies of the most hardened explorer. Eventually I find a method for trapping the wildly bucking hose against some body parts and making the best of a bad job.

It would be reassuring to find that others have experienced the same problem and that it's not just me. But I decide on reflection, if over breakfast I should bump into the only other hosteller that I've spoken to, asking Sonia about her time in the shower might not be the wisest start to the day.

As it happens, I arrive in the dining room on the dot of 7:30 as it opens for business and I have it to myself. It's colourful, simple and smart with a great view through the picture window of a canal basin, boats and an array of bridges: rail, road and a modern foot-bridge. The rain that briefly tired itself out is clearly not far away. And the fry up is as good as you'll get anywhere.

I have another detour to make before I can resume my walk, and it can only take place on a Friday. I need to be at Stockport railway station by 9:22 this morning to catch a train to Stalybridge. If I miss it there won't be another before the same time next Friday; hence my early breakfast and departure from the hostel to catch a train from Oxford Road to Stockport.

Known to *the cognoscenti* as a parliamentary train, or more colloquially as a ghost train, it runs because it has to and because nobody has got around to stopping it. Time was when the run from Stockport to Stalybridge was very useful for those travelling from the south and wanting to connect to trains from Manchester crossing the Pennines into Yorkshire. Making the connection in Manchester was a palaver as it required a hop across the city centre from one rail terminus to another, so the Stockport-Stalybridge connection provided a handy shortcut. But since the Trans Pennine trains now leave the same Manchester Piccadilly station as the route from the south via Stockport, there is little need for the connecting line. For Network Rail, the cost of formally withdrawing the service (closure notices, dealing with objections, and so on) would be greater than the costs of operating the weekly train, and so it lingers on – and since 1992 at its present minimal level – which makes it a favourite amongst a certain kind of person…

As the train before – a very run of the mill one, I feel – leaves the platform at Stockport (from which, incidentally, I can look down on the registry office where Mrs A and I tied the knot a while back), I look around to see if I can spot my fellow travellers and detect any sense of mounting anticipation. I'm discomforted to notice that I'm wearing a grey beard, an anorak (purely on account of the appalling weather) and a pair of what my wife has told me look very like Hush Puppies, and I'm carrying a bottle of water and a cardboard cup of station coffee which could be mistaken at a distance for a thermos.

I sidle up to a middle-aged woman who's about to board the 9:22 two coach train with me, make a supreme effort to appear normal and quietly ask if she's here for "the special train". Thankfully she doesn't seem too worried by me, but it transpires that Karen (for such is her name) is here because, well, she's in Stockport and needs to get to Stalybridge by train and has no idea what I'm talking about. She seems fairly relaxed and feigns interest in what I proceed to tell her – she may feel this is her safest option, there's a guard on board and the journey should only take 21 minutes.

With us in our carriage there's a young girl with headphones on connected to her mobile, and I decide she's not one of us and is best left. Our two other travelling companions have struck up a train-related conversation. On detecting possible kindred interest, the one with bobble hat and scarf and wearing a rucksack detaches himself to join Karen and me. His name is Tim and he hands me a printed slip of paper bearing the address of his own website *theghoststationhunters* which can point the curious (and you can take that whichever way you like) to any number of similar routes and services. Later, I log on and, in truth, it's fascinating. It probably helps if you have an interest in trains, social or industrial history, maps or just the downright quirky, and you're male.

We stop at Reddish South and Denton stations, the only train that does that all week. In the circumstances, the beautifully stocked and maintained planters on the platform at the former – courtesy of the Friends of Reddish South Station – are nothing short of heroic.

During the brief but intense conversation with Tim, I'm surprised to hear that he's married but less surprised when he tells us that he's done this run "loads of times" and he waxes particularly lyrical about a fortnight in the early days of the train's decline when the weekly service ran in both directions.

Karen is interested, or polite, enough to say that a ticket would make an ideal birthday or Christmas present for her husband – especially when I tell her that, with my Wrinkly Person's discount, it cost me £2.65.

As we disembark at Stalybridge we see one other passenger getting out of the second carriage who must have joined at one of the intervening stops. I'm pleased to see that he has the requisite grey beard, is carrying a rucksack and wears a bobble hat and bright red anorak.

I need to take a train back into the centre of Manchester to catch the tram out to Sale. There's snow on the hillsides around Stalybridge, it's pouring with rain and freezing cold on the platform. Because my day is to be spent zigzagging across Manchester – and I'm due to end up this evening not far from the youth hostel where I spent last night – I have cleverly decided to leave my rucksack behind in one of the lockers at the youth hostel, so I won't have to carry it all day, which means that I now have no access to the four or five extra layers of clothing so urgently needed.

I change to the tram at Piccadilly. In the years since I worked in the city there has been a transformation around the station on a par with Castlefield's regeneration. I must be frowning at the ticket machine for too long as a member of staff comes over to help. I hop onto the first tram and head confidently towards Salford

Quays and Media City. Which is a pity, as that's not the right line.

Even on the tram I'm shivering. I get off at a stop called Ice Station Zebra, or, strictly speaking, Exchange Quays, in order to catch a tram back to Cornbrook where I can switch to the correct line. With no shelter and seemingly no trams in that direction, I detect the onset of hypothermia. By the time I reach Sale, where my old colleague Mac is waiting for me, my teeth are chattering audibly.

We arrive at Sale Water Park where I have arranged to meet up again with Edward, my ex-colleague and landscape architect who showed me around the coastal nature reserve at Speke. The water park was one of the biggest projects that I worked on during my time at GMC and Edward was my partner in crime. He appears through the driving rain and sleet, dressed for a few months' sledge pulling to the South Pole. He has been checking on the trees that we planted forty years ago, and I'm happy to take his word for it.

Greater Manchester Council, through its brief twelve-year life from 1974 to 1986, ran a highly successful environmental programme of which the massive transformation of the county's semi-derelict river valleys was the keystone. We were responsible for: the planting of a million trees a year from our own tree bank (one of Mac's jobs); reclaiming spoil heaps into farmland, parks or industrial sites; and, in the case of Sale Water Park, converting a steep-sided motorway "borrow pit" or quarry into a busy sports venue complete with pathways, wildlife habitats, café and visitor centre. It now has its own tram stop. It wasn't a bad way to start my professional career.

My plan was to walk around the park with Edward and Mac, have lunch with them, then continue my walk from Sale along the Bridgewater Canal into the city centre. I manage the lunch, so that's one out of three…

I feel extremely inappropriately dressed, I'm visibly shivering and decide to call it a day. If the weather, and I, improve by morning, I can make up for it then. But now Mac drives me back to the hostel in Castlefield to retrieve the rucksack, then delivers me to tonight's accommodation south of the city centre, at the bottom end of Curry Mile.

The Partnership for Theological Education has provided, at Luther King House, a handy base for two days' exploration of Manchester at a price similar to the youth hostel. Nothing seems to be expected of me in terms of singing or soul searching.

I've had a good night's sleep. Some strange noises come from the wash basin this morning but there's a sachet of shampoo, so no risk of harmful residues. There's no locker, but if you can't trust these people...

There's a text from my daughter asking what the maximum fine is for being caught speeding and not having renewed your licence. It is good for both of us that I am 200 miles away.

The accommodation is in low-rise blocks around a cloistered courtyard and very tranquil – which I suppose is the idea – in a busy urban area. On the way to the breakfast room I call in to the library. It's massive and looks well organised and stocked with (what was I expecting?) Christian and ethical books and magazines, and well furnished with computer terminals.

There's a good, mainly cold, buffet spread for breakfast. Guests drift in solo or in middle-aged/elderly couples and keep themselves to themselves, unlike at the youth hostel. A young lady at reception tells me that much of their business comes from people like me – it turns out that she doesn't mean suave men-of-the-world so much as casual visitors looking for a low-cost stay rather than spiritual enlightenment. I notice snowflakes falling in the courtyard.

Mac has kindly offered to collect me and drop me back at Sale as I need to walk the bit that I failed to manage yesterday. There's a choice of routes from the water park: it would have been tempting to walk eastwards along the banks of the Mersey to Stockport then up the Tame valley to Ashton and Stalybridge, which would have taken me past many of the environmental projects that I'd cut my working teeth on, but I've opted to continue along the towpath of the Bridgewater Canal into Manchester city centre.

I'm not very digital when it comes to maps so I'm carrying the relevant 1:25,000 Ordnance Survey maps on each stage of the walk and today I have a copy of the Manchester A to Z. This probably marks me out from, say, Ranulph Fiennes.

The sun comes out and I'm enjoying the walk. I congratulate myself on the decision to postpone this stretch from yesterday – as if there had been a choice. The towpath here is well maintained and busy with cyclists, dogwalkers and self-loathing joggers. There are swans and Canada geese, which is good, as I can identify them. This is what my walk is supposed to be like. I pass anglers, and a rowing four, and narrow boats, one moored with the name *Juschillin* painted on the side.

To celebrate this turn for the better (I wonder if this will be my first day without rain) I stop, put down my rucksack and remove my thermal vest. At which point I hear a first clap of thunder.

I reach the Watch House Cruising Club on the towpath between Sale and Stretford, and learn that this building was once a staging post for packet boats to change horses. The information board shows an advertisement on the wall of the Watch House, for Macdonalds' Pottery Teeth, made by a local dentist. There isn't a date but I'm guessing they're not still trading. I'm pleased to see that the club sells JW (John Willy) Lees's range of beers. In my distant CAMRA membership days, the county of Greater Manchester was referred to in the annual Good Beer Guides as the Beer Drinker's Mecca (which, when I think of it now, seems a highly inappropriate expression). John Willy's was one of the county's traditional real ale brewers, having been at it since 1828, and is still brewing today in Middleton, north east of Manchester.

The rain that was threatening arrives in force. I stuff everything, apart from me, deep into plastic bags inside the rucksack, and press on. It's now pouring. A jogger passes but he's clearly spooked by a few Canada geese on the towpath and seeks my help in negotiating them. There are kayakers on the canal – I don't suppose it matters how wet they get. A granny on a tricycle is approaching, holding the lead of an equally elderly mongrel as they work their way slowly along the canal.

I pass a Staffordshire Bull Terrier – a Staffy – which I'm delighted to hear is called Wayne, so I know I must be getting near to Manchester United's ground at Old Trafford. In truth the similarity is a marked one.

Heavy duty graffiti covers the next info board that I pass in Crossford, so I can't tell you about the farm and school that used to be here – perhaps it was a disenchanted pupil or milkmaid.

The rain seems to be easing to a drizzle, or sleet, or perhaps it's a mild hail – is that even a thing? Very miserable anyway. I reach Waters Meeting where one branch of the Bridgewater heads northwest into Lancashire, the other into Manchester city centre. Checking my map proves worthwhile; I was heading in the wrong direction.

A narrow boat passes with a small white terrier on board and it makes me think of our recently departed Molly, half black Labrador, half fish. I'm wondering if I could have devised a coast to coast route which I might have walked while Molly swam the entire route alongside. Or perhaps a canal boat holiday with my wife – would our marriage survive that kind of challenge?

A pair of Canada geese drift by, accompanied by five fluffy goslings. I know there are five, but do they? I'm sure I heard somewhere – it was probably on *QI* – that ducks can't count above two, so do Canada geese use the same numerical system as our British ducks? Or do they bring their alien maths with them? A subject for a PhD, surely.

As I move further into Old Trafford, the path is increasingly soiled by goose droppings, dog mess, human litter and dereliction. But the drizzle makes for attractive patterns on the surface of the canal. Then there's no way – much as I might wish as a lifelong Liverpool FC nut – to avoid passing Manchester United's ground so I cross myself as the Sir Alex Ferguson stand dominates the view.

As I stand looking across the canal to the Old Trafford ground I'm mindful that Colin, an old colleague of mine, as bonkers about Man U as I am about Liverpool, emailed me a few days ago in response to the outcome of the Hillsborough inquest. Just four days ago, on 26 April, after the longest jury trial in British history, the second coroner's inquest into the 1989 Hillsborough disaster announced its findings, exonerating Liverpool fans and laying the responsibility – as those involved had always known – where it belonged: on the shoulders of the football authorities, the emergency services and particularly the South Yorkshire Police.

Whatever the media and politicians had said in the aftermath, the fans had not arrived drunk and forced their way into the ground for an FA Cup semi-final, they hadn't looted or urinated on the bodies of victims. Through the untiring efforts of the relatives, survivors and the implicit support of the whole city, the truth of the fatal organisational errors and the appalling institutional cover-up that followed, has at last emerged.

Why is this important? Because the ninety-six fans who went

to watch a football match in May 1989 and did not come home weren't the unfortunate victims of some awful accident: they were "unlawfully killed", meaning that individuals and organisations were responsible and needed to be accountable; and because the victims themselves were, for so long, held to be the guilty parties.

From where I sit – as a native of the city, lifetime supporter and long-time season ticket holder at Anfield, and now an ex-pat northerner living in the south – when the inquest findings were announced I felt proud of the city of my birth. I don't think this story would have developed in the same way elsewhere. Perhaps in some supposedly nicer location with less "baggage" than Liverpool there would not have been such a swift assumption of fan misbehaviour; there would have been less inclination on the part of the authorities to organise such a cover-up of historic proportions; and lastly there might not have been the determination and community cohesion amongst the wronged to see it through.

The rival Everton Football Club described the outcome as the greatest victory in the history of football. Colin, the Man U fan, had said something similar and I wasn't going to argue. Football clubs and their fans have their deep-seated rivalries, but some things run deeper.

I cross to the other side of the canal at Throstle Nest Bridge. I glance back once more towards the Temple of Doom and am pleased to see very black clouds gathering over Old Trafford... This is still Manchester United after all...

Suddenly a view opens up of the Manchester Ship Canal. The sky threatens and there's not enough blue to make a sailor a pair of trousers. There's a rowing eight and a single sculler, and a tram approaching Pomona station, crossing the canal above a small lock on its way to Eccles. Runners, joggers, walkers with Nordic poles. To my right the standard gauge railway with both goods and passenger trains, and the Bridgewater Canal which I've been following. Far in the distance the tall buildings of the city centre and new canal side apartments; in the middle ground dockside industry, cranes and warehousing; in the foreground some "economy scale" political graffiti and the detritus of abandoned commercial activity.

This may not be the prettiest landscape in Britain and I don't think my Aunty Win would have enthused, but somehow it's magnificent; a wide horizon with so much of our industrial, transport and social history spread before me, "in which every man has a right and interest who has an eye to perceive and a heart to enjoy" – as I just know Wordsworth would have said if he'd devoted a little less time to flowering spring bulbs and a little more to the joys of Salford and Trafford Park.

Further along the towpath past more Canada geese with four downy offspring, I pass warehouses still derelict, others already converted to hotels and apartments with balconies, all taking advantage of proximity to the water which until recently they would have turned their back on. This is urban living in the late 20th and early 21st centuries, and at last we've reached the centre of Manchester.

My first target is Sunlight House in Quay Street, the location of my first post-uni job as a town planner, and, when I worked there in the early 1970s, a nearly empty, seriously tired art deco 1930s "skyscraper". Occasionally, on returning from a lengthy Friday pub lunch (I think every day was Friday when I was there), we would dare each other to enter the unlit basement where, it was said, a crumbling swimming pool stood empty. The pool is now the heart of an upmarket spa and health club and the ground floor has long been occupied by the Old Grapes pub, once frequented by soap stars and Manchester United players and visited in a number of scenes by TV detectives Scott and Bailey. While writing this,

I'm surprised and disappointed (in the vernacular of the *Daily Telegraph* letters page), to read that the Grapes is no more, having been sacrificed in August in favour of a new reception area for the offices above.

But the place is busy enough when I arrive in April, planning to have lunch there for nostalgic reasons. Unfortunately, I fall foul of the queuing system at the bar, wander backwards and forward in an attempt to work out where and how to place my order and am eventually rejected as I haven't arrived at the front of the queue complete with table number. I decide to try somewhere simpler and eat a decent meat and potato pasty in Greggs who seem to know what their customers want.

In the afternoon, I'm spoilt for choice in terms of places to visit. I've only recently been to the Museum of Science and Industry at the old Liverpool Road station, the Lowry Centre in Salford Quays and Imperial War Museum North across the Ship Canal (temporary exhibition: "Fashion on the Ration: how to make a nice jumper out of dried egg and old bits of shrapnel"). But it's been a few years since I've visited one of my favourites – the People's History Museum, and it's just along the road.

This institution began life with a collection of Trades Union banners in the Mechanics' Institute in Princess Street; the birthplace not only of the TUC but also the Co-operative Insurance Society and the University of Manchester Institute of Science and Technology (UMIST). Now the museum (describing itself as the national museum of democracy), is based in an old pumping station on the edge of the city centre and covers such topics as: popular radicalism; Manchester's very own Peterloo Massacre; the Tolpuddle Martyrs and the history of trade unionism; the co-operative movement and friendly societies; women's suffrage; gay rights; the 1945 general election; the welfare state – and football.

The city's own role in these movements is highlighted: I'll be visiting Emmeline Pankhurst's house on my walk.

I regret having dropped history at school. I always knew I'd been born a geographer and at my school it was hard to do both subjects. The stuff I had covered, once we'd moved on from the Stone Age and Ancient Egypt, seemed to be largely about kings and queens and how much the world benefitted from British inputs. That doesn't really do enough for me these days. I've become increasingly interested in "the long march of everyman" and the faltering progress of society's rank and file around the globe. The people and projects that I'm keen to visit on my walk may be unheralded in some quarters but their efforts seem to me to be the very stuff of history. And the People's History Museum in Manchester, and others like the People's Palace in Glasgow, do a fine job of bringing that story to life.

From the window in the museum, I can see the Mark Addy pub on the opposite, Salford, bank of the River Irwell. It looks in a state and a helpful attendant tells me that it's done for, that severe flood damage has put paid to what was a very popular pub. I well recall it opening in 1980 and used to be a regular customer.

Mac has driven into town to meet me at the museum and take me to see one or two important cultural icons on the south side of the city centre.

Our first port of call is the Vimto sculpture in Granby Row. Vim Tonic, as it was originally, was first distilled (I prefer "discovered") on this site in 1908 from the juice of grapes, raspberries and blackcurrants, flavoured with herbs and spices, exploiting a market generated by the temperance movement. I find it deeply reassuring to know that it's available as an ice lolly, in slush form and on draught as well as in bottles and cans. And apparently it goes down massively, and frequently, in Saudi Arabia, Gambia and Senegal. The 1992 sculpture – a giant sized bottle surrounded by

Vimto's constituent fruits in proportion – hadn't coped well with Manchester weather and the attention of students but returned home in 2011 after a painstaking, loving restoration.

From here it's a short walk to Sackville Gardens and the statue of Alan Turing, the wartime codebreaker who continued work as a proto-computer boffin after the war. The Gardens are occupied by the Manchester May Day Festival, a date with particular significance for the labour movement. There's a programme of talks and events both here and in the Mechanics' Institute, and an array of stalls promoting such as: CND; the British Medical Association; the National Union of Journalists; Salford Community Theatre; the Friends of the Manchester Peace Gardens; the NHS; the UNITE union; and a campaign on food waste. It's like an alfresco People's History Museum this afternoon. Alan Turing is currently holding a "Cameron Must Go" placard.

We move on to Victoria Park a mile or two south. Once an upmarket residential suburb (home to Charles Halle, Ford Madox Brown and Elizabeth Gaskell, and where the Pankhursts lived before Emmeline's husband died and she moved to cheaper accommodation closer into town), Victoria Park has been designated a conservation area. Many of the properties are in multi-occupation and in need of some loving care – I know, I lived in one for a few years in the mid-1970s and the area was rundown then. Which is how I, as a recent graduate, could afford to live there.

We call in at a church designed for the Christian Scientists by Edgar Wood around 1906 but looking much younger. Wood was an innovative, flamboyant local architect who would turn up for work wearing a large black cloak lined with red silk and a flat, broad-brimmed hat and brandishing a silver handled cane. His church in Victoria Park owed much to the Arts and Crafts movement of William Morris. Built in partly rendered brick with a steeply pitched roof, it has an entrance under a semi-circular arch and a front window shaped like a cross. There are two wings, one in the form of a turret with a conical roof.

Pevsner considered it "the only religious building in Lancashire that would be indispensable in a survey of twentieth century church design in all England." It's Grade I listed, and gorgeous.

The church closed in 1971 and was heavily vandalised (that's the area I was living in) before reopening as the Edgar Wood Centre in 1975. In turn, this closed in 2003, and the building is currently used by the Universal Church of the Kingdom of God. Mac and I find the door unlocked and begin a tour of the inside. We're soon joined by a very friendly pastor (if that's how they're titled) more than happy to chat about the building, its congregation and links with the community. This seems to chime with the focus of my walk on community engagement but when our host proclaims the successes of the church in converting people of other faiths I'm on uncertain territory and it's time to move on.

From here it's a short walk to my former residence from the mid-1970s. I see they've got the builders in, and about time. I retain one particular memory from when I lived here. I had been out on the Saturday to a friend's wedding, where youngsters kept coming up to my table to ask the chap next to me for his autograph. It seemed only polite to ask who or what he was. His name, he said, was Tony Wilson and he worked as a reporter and presenter on the north west news programme for ITV. (I think I was a BBC man and anyway to get reception I had to stand alongside my portable TV holding the aerial above my head and I didn't regard regional telly as a priority). Tony became known as Mister Manchester for, amongst other things, co-founding Factory Records and setting up the Hacienda club…

Anyway, the next morning as usual I was asleep in the kitchen, feeling the effects of a late, emotional Saturday night. I shared a three-room flat – that's three including the kitchen – with two others, all of us in our early twenties, and this arrangement avoided the need to share a room. I woke on hearing my door being opened. A middle-aged woman walked in, made no sign that she was aware of me, headed to the oven in the corner where she filled the kettle and put it on to boil, and then left. In my befuddled state I wasn't sure what just happened. I seemed to be in my own place. I had no idea who this woman was, but she looked like she belonged. Although I'd clearly had more to drink than was wise I didn't believe I'd met this lady last night. Perhaps if I closed my eyes things would look clearer. I dozed.

Five minutes later the door opened again, the same woman reappeared (I thought, I almost hoped, it was the same woman), revisited the kettle, made something with it and departed, again without a glance in my direction. She may have had two mugs in her hand, but I couldn't work through the implications.

I dozed again. Perhaps, if I could just sleep through the day, everything would turn out alright.

About half an hour later the woman reappeared carrying bowls of rhubarb and settled herself at my – yes, my – table. Not a word had yet been exchanged. Was it down to me to say something? Might she be dangerous? Are these folk best left until the proper authorities are informed?

The door opened once more, and a younger woman entered, and also sat at the table. There was something vaguely familiar about this one, but I couldn't place her. Was she at the wedding? She said something. She sounded Scottish and was looking in my direction. I tried hard to focus but felt at a social disadvantage under my duvet. She appeared to be smiling, which was reassuring, and I started to pick out words. Pieces started to fall into place. This, it seemed, was one of the people who, weeks earlier, had come to the flat in response to my advert about a room being available. In those far-off days she had apparently communicated with me by the only available method – a letter – that she planned to take up the place this weekend, with her mother's help. Her letter arrived the following week.

It wasn't a great start. We've been best friends for over 40 years and, as Helen, she makes several appearances in this narrative.

I'm starting to flag, and Mac returns me to the Luther King House from where this evening I'm due to meet up with three more ex-GMC chums on Curry Mile, excluding Mac unfortunately, who has unaccountably allowed a family gathering to take precedence.

Rusholme's run of Indian and Bangladeshi restaurants, a very short stroll from my accommodation, has grown since I lived nearby and now has its own signposting and marketing by the City Council. Thanks to my friends' local knowledge we've booked one of the best and our meal, following a swift one in the Albert Inn, is what I've looked forward to all day. We're quite late into the evening when one of our party announces, "I must tell you an interesting story about my collection of Irish train tickets." It's time to head back to Martin Luther's place for the night.

Chapter 5

Suffragettes and the Taj Mahal of Swimming

Luther King House gives me a second decent night's sleep though I resorted to the ear plugs, not because of other guests but because there are strange central heating type noises from somewhere. At breakfast there are youngsters as well as the older singles and couples who were around yesterday. And when I set off there's a live band (what other sort is there?) practising what sound like modern churchy songs.

After stopping first to take pictures of the Toast Rack – I still love it – I head to an equally iconic building from another era. I've been friends with this one for a while too – literally a "friend", as in Friends of Victoria Baths. The baths opened to the public in 1906, not only with three Olympic-size swimming pools (Men's First Class or Gala, Men's Second Class and Women's – with its own surviving spittoons, how nice) but also "slipper baths" for washing and a suite of Turkish baths. Soon known as the Water Palace – and described in *Great Lengths* (English Heritage's guide to the historic indoor swimming pools of Britain) as the "Taj Mahal of British Swimming", it stood out even amongst the fine public baths being built in the Edwardian era in the city and elsewhere. It's a stunning picture of rich terracotta, art nouveau stained glass, sumptuous green tiles and mosaics.

You may not want to read that the water for the pools was

recycled from the First Class Men's pool to the Second Class, and then to the Women's, but you would be impressed with the list of national swimming champions who swam here and the variety of uses to which the facilities were put – there are entire books devoted to the baths' importance to the 20th century dance scene.

My contact with the baths in the 1970s, when I lived within walking distance, was limited to one or two failed attempts to learn to swim, or even take my feet off the bottom. In truth, while I love buildings like this one, I have never found cold, austere swimming baths inviting in their basic purpose and eventually learned to swim in my thirties in modern leisure centres in the Moss Side and Stretford areas of Manchester. I made more frequent visits to the Turkish element of the Victoria Baths to be steam cleaned and pummelled by eunuchs. (That last bit may be a product of false memory syndrome but if so it's a vivid one.)

After moving away from the area, I can't say that the baths loomed large in my consciousness until I spotted them one day in 2003 being paraded for public voting to receive major lottery funding via the BBC's Restoration programme. Never having voted previously for much besides politicians or Trade Union reps, not even to give some unknown celebrity the chance to eat kangaroo testicles, I nevertheless moved myself, along with 282,000 other viewers, to act and was well pleased to see the baths net the big one. The runaway margin of victory may suggest that non-Mancunians, apparently voting in large numbers in support, were reminded by the programme of the much-loved baths they had lost from their own communities.

This windfall was, of course, only the start and an irrepressible team of volunteers has laboured long, first to safeguard the building from the elements, and then to attract sufficient funds to bring the Turkish baths and at least one of the pools back into business. The baths have, for a while now, been open for weddings, fairs, markets, musical and theatrical events and continue to attract interest and support.

Barry, a long-time volunteer on the project and now one of the trustees, has agreed to meet me at the baths this morning just before the start of one of their open days. He introduces me to some of the team of eight volunteers working on the wonderful stained-glass windows – they have some paid staff working on restoration work and fundraising but much of the activity resides with volunteers. They're from a range of backgrounds; some have jobs, others are students on temporary projects.

Barry mentions a long-term ambition to see the baths develop as a national museum of swimming. They deserve to get there.

I need to head into the city centre before turning east towards the Pennines and I've something like twelve miles to do today. En route, and just five minutes' walk away from Victoria Baths, is the neo-classical villa in Plymouth Grove where Elizabeth Gaskell lived from 1850 until her death in 1865.

With so much of the area having been subject to slum clearance and redeveloped for low-rise new housing in the 1960s, the villa stood out when I lived nearby as something of an oddity. Although known to have been the home of the author of *Cranford*, *North and South*, and *Wives and Daughters*, it wasn't open to the public. It was locally referred to as the Pink House owing – no surprise – to its lurid colouring when it was owned by Manchester University and housed the International Society. Happily, the house was purchased in 2004 by the Manchester Historic Buildings Trust. Restoration work began in 2009 and, despite a major setback when its brand-new lead roof was stolen two years later, the house opened to the public in 2014.

Having passed the place so often when I lived in Victoria Park and there was no public access, I've arranged my walk this morning to be here on a Sunday when it will be open. Like the baths, the Gaskell House is a rare surviving architectural and historic gem in an area generally past its best which might well have been lost if not for lottery funding and impressive voluntary effort.

I'm first obliged to admire the gardens – partly because they are attractively set out and look well-tended and partly because they are the responsibility in a voluntary capacity of my ex-colleague Edward who has already shown me around the Speke coastal reserve and Sale Water Park on this trek.

I'm greeted this morning by another Elizabeth, a trustee of the House and a member of the Elizabeth Gaskell Society long before the property came into its present hands. She tells me that the writer was a favourite of hers when she studied English Literature at school, that Gaskell was then an underrated author and a better narrator of working class life than Charles Dickens.

This was apparently the Gaskells' third house in the area as they gradually moved outwards from the city centre as the family grew, Plymouth Grove being then a salubrious, tree-lined avenue on the edge of Victoria Park with fields to either side. Visitors to the house included Dickens, John Ruskin, Charlotte Bronte, Harriet Beecher Stowe, and Charles Halle when he came to give piano lessons, which isn't bad. "That Charlotte Bronte's been round again, says she's had it up to here with their Bramwell – oh, and Harriet Beecher Stowe asks if we're doing anything this Saturday?"

Elizabeth claims that their room volunteers are "more tactile than the National Trust". I think she means that I'm encouraged to touch stuff if I want to, not that I'm likely to be groped. She tells me that the house balances its books but that the current round of lottery funding – which pays the salaries of the house manager and the part-time education officer – will run out in 18 months. There is solid income from admissions, sales, the tearoom and filming but they are vulnerable to any major building repairs which might come along, and additional cash would have to be found for any growth, such as a study centre in the conservatory.

I do my bit for the budget with a tasty piece of St Clement's pie and a coffee in a nice cup and saucer. Anything in a cardboard cup would just look wrong...

To make me feel at home, the rain is coming down again as I walk north towards the Mancunian Way flyover. This is familiar territory to me, the short journey from my old flat-share in Victoria Park into the city centre, but in the years since I lived here much of "downtown" has undergone a transformation. Manchester University and the Royal Infirmary have been here longer than I can remember but their campuses just south of the city centre have expanded beyond recognition. I look briefly inside the sparkly Aquatics Centre, built for the 2002 Commonwealth Games where terraced housing used to be. I wonder if, like the Victoria Baths, it will attract its own nostalgic fan club if and when it starts showing its age.

Amongst the few older buildings in the area to have survived are a pair of Victorian villas, 60 and 62 Nelson Street, standing discordantly on their own plot in what is now the city's hospital quarter. Number 62 was the home for over eight years of Emmeline Pankhurst who moved her family here from Victoria Park, down-sizing after the death of her husband, Richard. In 1903 this house was the birthplace of the Suffragette movement.

By 1979, the house had fallen into disrepair and the North West Health Authority applied for permission to demolish both 60 and 62 Nelson Street. The application produced a storm of protest from women's groups and from conservationists. Permission to demolish was refused and the Health Authority agreed to lease the houses to the Pankhurst Trust, established to restore the buildings and put them back into public use as the Pankhurst Centre.

Restoration work started in 1984. Labour was recruited through Community Programme Schemes to ensure that women were employed on the site and the Centre was formally opened three years later by Emmeline's great-granddaughter, Helen, and Barbara Castle on the anniversary of the first meeting of the Suffragettes.

I can see it, I can walk around the outside, but I can't get in, not today. The Centre only opens to the public on Thursdays and, try as I might in planning my itinerary, I haven't been able to combine the Centre, Mrs Gaskell and an open day at the Victoria Baths into one day. This is why I took the opportunity of a trip to Manchester earlier in the spring and arranged to meet one of the volunteers here.

In 1903, the first meeting of the Women's Social and Political Union was held here at number 62, the Pankhursts' house. The WSPU took on the role of a more militant element of the broader suffragist movement and was led by Emmeline and her daughters Christabel, Sylvia and Adela. Recognising the value of imagery, and what we might now call branding, the WSPU adopted a distinctive purple, white and green colour scheme symbolising dignity, purity and hope respectively and used it for banners, flags, rosettes and badges. It was a WSPU scarf, or possibly a flag or sash, that Emily Wilding Davison attempted, during the 1913 Derby, to attach to the bridle of the King's horse, Anmer, when she lost her life in the cause.

While Emmeline and Christabel called a halt to the WSPU programme of direct action for the duration of WW1 and supported conscription and the war effort, Sylvia was fiercely opposed to Britain's involvement in the war. She sought closer links between suffragism and the Labour movement, saw gaining the vote as one element in a broader struggle against financial, class, gender and racial inequalities and based herself increasingly in London's East End amongst its working women. A gulf appeared between her work and Emmeline and Christabel's reliance on educated, middle class women as campaigners and their absolute focus on "the vote" as the panacea. It was consistent with her approach that Sylvia was the only Pankhurst actually to undergo the horrors of forcible feeding when imprisoned in Holloway for smashing an undertaker's window. As her politics continued to shift to the left, she founded the short-lived Communist Workers Party. After she gave birth to a son at the age of forty-five and declined to marry the father, Emmeline never spoke to her again. Sylvia took up the cause of Ethiopian independence from Italy and became close to Emperor Haile Selassie. At his invitation she moved to Addis Ababa in 1956. When she died in 1960 aged 78, she received a full state funeral and was proclaimed an "Honorary Ethiopian".

The third daughter, Adela, also opposed Britain's involvement in WW1, fell out with the WSPU, emigrated to Australia in 1914 and was a founding member of the Communist Party of Australia. By the mid-1920s she had become disillusioned with communism and founded the anti-communist Australian Women's Guild of Empire. In 1941 she was a founding member of the right wing, nationalistic Australia First Movement and was arrested and interned for advocating peace with Japan.

All of which suggests there may be more than one blockbuster movie to be made from the story of this one extraordinary Manchester family.

The Centre houses displays, books, documents and films about the Pankhursts, suffragism, other historic moments in the fight for social and gender equality, and Manchester's considerable place in those movements and their continuing relevance today. Current news items in this country and abroad will demonstrate how far we still have to travel – a century since women over 30 were granted the vote by the 1918 Representation of the People Act – in terms of the way women are treated. As well as hosting an important historical and archival record, it serves as a women's community centre, providing space for activities and events run by women, for women, with the mission:

> To ensure that the powerful story of the women who won the vote continues to inspire those who dare to challenge gender inequality and the violence and social injustice this fosters.
>
> To work to ensure that people suffering, or at risk of, domestic abuse receive appropriate support.

Plans are nearing completion for a statue of Emmeline to be erected in Manchester in 2019 – on International Women's Day. London already has one; it's time that the city of her birth, her home for 50 years and the birthplace of the Suffragettes, followed suit. Hitherto if you were a woman you more or less had to be Queen Victoria to be commemorated by a statue, but we move forward. Very much involved in the plans for the statue and its unveiling is Helen Pankhurst, great-granddaughter of Emmeline, granddaughter of Sylvia and herself highly active in international development and women's rights. Helen's own daughter, Laura, appeared beside her in the 2012 London Olympic Games opening ceremony and in cameo roles in the 2015 film *Suffragette* and is clearly cut of the family cloth. As I say, an extraordinary family.

I pass under the Mancunian Way flyover with its plaque, "Concrete Society Award 1968". TONE and KEV have added one or two thoughts of their own by means of a spray gun in a large, unfamiliar font. It's late Sunday morning and the city centre is quiet in the steady rain.

Canal Street has been the heart of gay Manchester for several decades and now bears its own branding and signs: "Manchester's Gay Village: Enjoy Yourself Responsibly". In this weather, at this hour, there's little to suggest anyone's enjoying themselves, responsibly or not. I'm feeling quite subdued, but I hear a text arrive and hunt around for my mobile: it's from my niece Nicky informing me that Liverpool are two nil down at Swansea and it's half time in today's early kick-off.

At the end of Canal Street, the towpath restarts, and I set off down a ramp which will take me underground for a short stretch near Piccadilly Station. I hesitate. There may well be people living down there and I suspect we may have little in common. Wandering through someone's sleeping arrangements may yield some interesting material but, on balance, I opt to return to the road and continue eastwards past New Islington.

This is not an expression that I recognise but it turns out to be the invented name for a rundown part of Ancoats being regenerated with the help of a new cut linking the Rochdale and Ashton canals, and involving the conversion of mills and warehouses to apartments and a new eight storey block conceived as "three fat chips stacked on top of each other".

I'm following the Ashton Canal. As I aim to be in Ashton tonight, this has a logic to it. I'm getting near to the stadium where, in 2002, I watched some of the track and field programme and the finish of the men's marathon in the Commonwealth Games. It's now the home of Manchester City FC and called the City of Manchester Stadium, if I ignore the name of its sponsors. It's to my right across the canal along with the National Squash Centre and the

Manchester Regional Arena, both dating from the 2002 Games.

It's still raining. Nicky texts again: Liverpool have had a player sent off and we're losing three-one. I thank her, but not in a nice way.

Near the entrance to Phillips Park the towpath switches to the other side of the canal. There's a view of the velodrome which, for once, wasn't built for the Commonwealth Games but eight years earlier and has been the home of British cycling ever since.

There are what look to be lower cost apartments overlooking the canal. One balcony has some very wet washing out to dry. It won't.

The first people I've seen for a while, two men, approach on the towpath. They're both shaven headed and look a bit scary until they get a bit nearer, when I see one is carrying a puppy in his arms and it's wearing a Santa Claus outfit, which seems unusual at this time of year.

Mallards with tiny ducklings. A moorhen. A heron. More bloody Canada geese. The male, I presume, is the one on the path telling me to keep my distance; the female is the one over there on the nest. I believe they're quite old-fashioned in that respect.

There are houses with gardens coming down to the canal on the far side, most with tables, chairs and a view. But others have sealed themselves off behind a high fence or a big shed.

I arrive at the Moravian Settlement in Fairfield and I take a step back in time to the late 18th century. The Moravian Church as a faith dates from the late 14th century. Its members took issue with some of the practices of the Roman Catholic Church and wanted to return the church in Bohemia and Moravia to what they believed were the simpler ways of early Christianity. These were some of the earliest Protestants, rebelling against Rome more than a hundred years before Martin Luther. I take shelter from the rain in the church during a service. A lady handing out hymn books tells me that Michael Portillo won't be far behind me or, at least, he'll be along in a few weeks. I won't wait.

The settlement, designated a conservation area since 1971, originally included an inn, shop and bakery as well as the church, schools for boys and girls, attractive brick built cottages and separate accommodation for unmarried men and women. The few streets are wide with mature trees, setts and cobbles and an ordered symmetry. There is a quietness and insularity – which is a pity today as I really fancy a cup of tea and a nice biscuit and there's nowhere. I presume when Mr. Portillo arrives in due course on his train to do his piece, he won't even have to ask for a cup of tea.

It seems the single brethren's house was not an unmitigated success. According to Mellowes', *A Short History of Fairfield Moravian Church,* "The young men were frequently admonished for drinking too much at the settlement's inn; on one occasion, they had some fun at a fire drill by turning the hosepipe on Brother Gilpin who took offence."

Single brethren, eh? What are they like?

I phone Eric, another former colleague from GMC, to let him know where I've reached as he lives not far away and has offered to give me moral support on the last stage of today's effort. He tells me that the tearoom at Portland Basin, where I plan to meet him, has just closed for the day. Some friend.

I eventually stagger into Ashton under Lyne where Eric is lurking – tealess, not even a thermos about his person – at the canal basin where the Ashton meets the Peak Forest and Huddersfield Canals. This last will be quite important over coming days and weeks as it will take me across the Pennines. Eric proves to me that the tearoom is definitely closed, and we press on along the Huddersfield Canal towards Stalybridge where I am promised beer aplenty, and possibly reasonable conversation (I'm feeling grumpy), on the station platform, oddly enough.

Eric informs me that much of the towpath from here is in rubbish condition. He's not wrong. We pass a good deal of rundown and derelict property: there doesn't seem to be much in the way of regeneration happening along this stretch.

In light drizzle, which is as good as it gets today, Eric and I arrive at the Station Buffet in Stalybridge. It looks full, which isn't a good look right now as far as I'm concerned. I've come a long way. Many of these people are waiting for a train to take them on a rail-based pub crawl. If I can't find a seat soon I'll be on somebody's knee.

Just in time a small opportunity arises, and I start rearranging furniture while Eric does the decent thing and battles through to the bar. Once I have my first pint inside me I can start to appreciate what is in fact a very attractive Victorian bar with fine original fittings, photographs of the station in its heyday and other memorabilia, and a most acceptable array of real ales. I'm looking forward to spending the rest of my life here. I've promised myself some traditional pub fare, or fayre. I like the sound of the black peas.

The man behind the marble-topped bar says, "If you'd been here a bit earlier, we had food on. See this group here – the ones on the pub trail? They ate it all. We've got salt and vinegar or scratchings."

We're joined by Mac (again) and Nick, another friend from work, and decide to concentrate on the beer. It's medically proven that you need to rehydrate after walking.

Eventually we decide it's curry time, which follows on naturally after an amiable session in the pub. These are the bits I've always liked best about walking. From here it's a taxi ride back into Ashton. (I've walked this part already in the other direction and

I'm not obliged to do it again, especially at night and especially not along *that* towpath.) Nick and I will be spending the night afloat, or at least moored, on *Hazel*, an old narrow boat, in Portland Basin.

Nick has been able to arrange this as an active member of the Wooden Canal Boat Society. I know I'll have the opportunity in the morning to ask him about all that. Tonight, it's just a case of climbing on board – not as easy as it might have been before today's hike and liquid-enhanced evening – and identifying the location of vital facilities before climbing into a borrowed sleeping bag. Tomorrow I'll be doing it all again. Zzzzzzz.

Birdsong is all very well in theory but not at dawn in early May, thank you, not through the leaky windows of a canal boat.

A slow start this morning, a shower. Nick has prepared generously, and we have the makings in kit form of a great cooked breakfast. As well as catching up with several years of family and social news, he reminds me that, when working for Liverpool City Council just before joining GMC, it was he who gave planning permission for the Shankly Gates at Anfield, commemorating Liverpool's most famous manager. Wish I had that on my CV.

I grill him about the Wooden Canal Boat Society.

It seems that a good number of the old friends and colleagues that I'm meeting up with, having retired or semi-retired from the paid stuff, are still working but without the money. In Nick's case he joined the Society thinking it would be quietly therapeutic to spend a few hours a week painting and varnishing in a good cause, but found himself doing committee work instead – for which he had plenty of experience but for which he retained little enthusiasm. But as far as I'm concerned, you can just never have enough meetings.

Hazel was born in Runcorn in 1914, built to carry coal and salt. She has changed hands many times since then and did a good deal of campaigning in the 1950s at boat rallies that helped to save the canal network from being closed. Known now as the *Wellbeing* boat, *Hazel* has undergone major restoration and provides waterway holidays for people recovering from stress, depression and other illnesses. She is towed by motor boats and occasionally by horse.

The Society experiences similar challenges to other projects that I've been visiting, particularly the continuing struggle for cash and human resources. How do you determine priorities between charities? I work for one with an environmental aim: the conservation of the landscape and wildlife of a national park. It's an important cause but any charitable cash contributions that I might make go elsewhere. Perhaps we're fortunate that people's passions differ so much.

Restoring an old canal boat, like rebuilding a steam engine or refurbishing a historic water wheel, is a worthwhile end in itself and there must be satisfaction and a sense of real achievement in that accomplishment whether you're employed or a volunteer. Being able to put that vehicle or machine to some social benefit as well is to be applauded, but competition for volunteer time and charitable funding in a crowded field is going to be an ongoing problem for many such causes. The Wooden Canal Boat Society is currently able to fund a Boat Manager, a Hazel Project Manager and a Volunteer Co-ordinator who amongst other tasks organises things like boat painting classes. They run a monthly recycling trip along the canal to Fairfield and Droylsden with the aim of selling some of the collected material on eBay or through the former Woolworths shop in Ashton. Nick tells me that this operation brings a lot more grit than oysters.

Some of the smaller charities who might wish to book the *Wellbeing* boat are increasingly short of funds, preventing them from being regular customers, which in turn affects *Hazel's* balance sheets. They had that John Sergeant on board not long ago, doing one of his TV programmes about canals, but the Society didn't feel they got what they hoped for in terms of financial contribution or a decent mention, and they need all the publicity they can get.

On board *Hazel* we're handily placed for Portland Basin Museum, a few yards away across the cobbled car park. It's housed in the attractively restored 19th century Ashton Canal Warehouse and tells the industrial and social history of the area. The last time I was here there was a special exhibition on the history, social and global significance of Vimto. I bought a large jigsaw of Vimto posters through the ages, which I still own. I haven't started it yet, but perhaps when there are no more meetings…

Now there's a 1920s street (I'm not sure you need to go to a museum to see one of those in Ashton) and displays on canals, mining, glove making, farming. And donkey stoning? It's OK, it involves cleaning your front step. The place is light and modern inside, simple, inviting, varied in its presentations – and free. On this May Bank Holiday Monday morning it's already busy.

Tameside Council, who run the museum, are apparently happy for *Hazel* and the Society's other boats moored here to serve as useful adjuncts to what's on display but the rather battered looking hulks still awaiting restoration work would benefit from some explanation and interpretation to show that they hadn't just been dumped there.

Nick's wife, Julie, has brought the car down to the Basin to collect Nick, and they drive me back to Stalybridge to resume my walk along the Huddersfield Canal. They drop me outside Tesco, handily placed alongside the canal, so I can pick up something "for the journey". It's still raining so picking up a 4X4 might have been useful.

On this trip, I've been very conscious of the role that water in general, and canals in particular, can play in revitalising rundown places. Stalybridge to some extent went downhill in recent years but it's now opening itself up to the canal again; there are new apartments taking advantage of the view.

Nick mentioned a site he wants me to look at on the far side of the canal, and now I can't miss it. It's a depot where his Society sorts the material collected on its recycling trips. To all intents and purposes, it looks like a junkyard and from this distance across the canal you'd be hard pressed to think of it as making a positive contribution to anything. It carries a large banner that reads, "Wooden Canal Boat Society: Volunteers Wanted". Nick doesn't feel this is the Society's best recruiting device and I'm inclined to agree.

I leave Stalybridge and walk north on the towpath into open country for the first time for a while. This is a farmed landscape but I'm walking through a narrow corridor of woodland. I can hear, and occasionally see, the River Tame running alongside – the canal builders selected its valley to provide the easiest route through the Pennine foothills. The canal locks look in good condition and water seems to be running in all the right places (that's my technical judgement coming into play).

An unfamiliar yellow object appears in the sky above. Now, this feels like proper walking.

They say you get to think great thoughts when you walk solo. I give it a try.

Mmm. Nothing yet.

No, still nothing.

Ah, here's one: "This is uphill. I thought canals were, well, flat." Generally speaking, following a canal should mean a gentler progress than clambering over open country but it still has to get over a bl**dy big range of hills so I guess it must go upwards, otherwise there wouldn't be any locks. That's not bad for a first go. I might give this "great thoughts" thing another go tomorrow, help pass the time.

I reach Scout Tunnel. There's an alternative route on offer across the top but a narrow, uneven, paved path follows the side of the canal through the tunnel. I go for the shorter route. It's extremely dark down here and I'm glad there's a handrail between me and a Missing Person's announcement. I'm nearly through before I remember that I put on my sunglasses shortly before coming into the tunnel.

Safely out the other side, I start seeing cyclists and dog walkers, and black Labradors actually in the canal near Mossley. More Canadas guarding their nests. A young couple apologise to me by one of the locks as their small child toddles across in front of me – does that mean I look "infirm"? Is that worse than being offered a seat on the Undergound?

Stone cottages, well-kept locks and fine views of the Pennines. Clouds pass – white, grey, black, keeping me on my toes, poised for costume change.

I'm slowly catching up with a hired narrow boat on which a rather alternative looking couple are playing a very loud and unpleasant soundtrack of some kind of music. Is that even legal? It's truly horrible. Do I, in grumpy old man mode, call out, "Oy, turn off that bloody racket!" or would it be more effective, to borrow loosely from *The Onion* publication, to explain that I do not need some riffraff cruising through my neighbourhood cranking deep cuts from the Booty Bar Records catalogue at such an ungodly volume with a tricked-out stereo blaring Bitch Ass Darius B-sides or classic tracks off Disco D's genre-epitomising album *Straight Out Tha Trunk*? Or some repetitive TR-808-driven regional electronic subgenre inspired by legendary Detroit DJ the Electrifying Mojo, to say nothing of polluting my ears with endlessly looping screwed-and-chopped vocals, multi-layered Euro-synthpop samples and complicated record-scratching techniques?

People passing along the towpath in the opposite direction are only briefly exposed to this cacophony. I'm travelling in the same direction and overtaking it at less than half a mile an hour. I'm not capable of sprinting and I'm very reluctant to follow my usual routine of pausing every so often to jot down any notes or I'll never get away from it. Head down and keep plodding. I remain silent but give them, you know, a look. They smile and wave back.

More picturesque locks, packhorse bridges. Mills converted into apartments. The sun shining on the heather moors up to my right. Some upmarket, new canal side properties in Greenfield and Uppermill with well-tended gardens – but built of brick! Here, in the Pennine foothills where houses are hewn from the solid stone? How did that happen? And here's a really repulsive new development with a large shared garden running down to the canal – what possessed the builders? Was it Friday afternoon in the planning office? (I'm allowed to say that…)

Most people you pass in areas like this, on days like this, will tend to say hello or give some sort of greeting. But one middle-aged chap, as we pass, proffers a gruff, unsolicited, "These cyclists have made a right ruddy mess of this, haven't they?" In reply I muster, "Erm, ha," which seems to do the trick.

The sun is quite warm now and, it being Bank Holiday Monday, there are plenty of people out on the towpath with dogs and pushchairs. At a canal side pub with a busy beer garden, everyone seems to be having a good time. I'm tempted but it seems a mistake to stop now, with the end almost in sight.

I leave the canal to walk down Uppermill's main street. The

Waggon Inn is not far along and that's where I'm booked in. A long, cold drink follows, as I sit at a table on the pavement. I'm happy and feel like I've earned it. It's a busy road and a lively looking place: shops, pubs and cafes doing good trade in the sunshine. All I have to do now is decide where to eat. The barman at the Waggon says they can't feed me after six o'clock as it's the Bank Holiday, this is Britain and the staff have had a busy day. He wants to know if they need to get someone to come in tomorrow to make breakfast for me. I don't plan to make my own.

My evening constitutional doesn't take me far. There's an excellent chippy almost next door that does me a fish supper with mushy peas and a buttered muffin. Uppermill looks gorgeous in the late sunshine with inviting side streets and well-kept public gardens and play areas. I'm due back here in a few weeks' time for the annual Saddleworth Brass Band Contests on Whit Friday so I track down where it's all going to take place and head back to the Waggon Inn.

As good as their word, the inn has arranged for a chef to come in just to make my breakfast at a time of my choosing. I come down at eight and a single table is set for me with a full menu choice. The breakfast is beautifully prepared. The chef also gives me tips on how to "do" both the Whit Friday event and the "Yanks" weekend in August, following in the spirit of the 1979 movie of that name with Richard Gere and Vanessa Redgrave which was filmed all around this area.

The Saddleworth Museum over the road, which has been recommended, has scaffolding all over it. I think the shop and information parts will be open from one till four today but that's no use to me. And it's started raining again, quite hard: rucksack off, bag cover fitted, hood up, and off we go. I'm getting good at this.

I'm aiming for the nearest railway station, at Greenfield. I pass a big sign at the side of the road saying, "Oldham: working for a co-operative borough" but I don't know what it means. The rain has changed to hail, but I won't be doing much walking today. I don't want to press on beyond Uppermill yet as I want to be back here for the brass band festival later this month.

The station is an attractive stone and slate affair, set against a backdrop of the Pennines which, in this downpour, look grey and bleak in contrast to their sunny, inviting appearance of yesterday afternoon. Living near the south coast I've become more used to the softness of the chalky South Downs, but I know just how forbidding the Pennines can be in bad weather.

The ticket office is staffed although there's just myself and one other person waiting. I'm going to Stalybridge to pick up a connection for home. She's waiting for a train in the other direction, towards Leeds. From her accent she's African but I can't pin it down. She says she's studying healthcare in Huddersfield and has a placement at a Leeds hospital. She lives in Delph and has taken a bus to get here, will take a train from Greenfield to Huddersfield then change for Leeds. Every day. I mention the gathering of the bands which I'm looking forward to, and she tells me she has two stepchildren who play in the Holmfirth and Middleton bands, that it's a great event and she'll look out for me.

For now, though, it's time I was heading back to Sussex to my day job. It's a good journey home on the train until London Victoria, from where a trip that should take one hour takes three. It's great to be back with Southern Rail.

Chapter 6

Brass Bands, Coal Mines and Canal Tunnels

It's Whit Friday, late May, and I'm back in Uppermill for the annual gathering of bands in the moorland towns and villages of Saddleworth in the Pennine foothills. This is by no means a new thing: the first record of the event is from 1884. Rain is forecast but is holding off.

My father was always a fan of brass band music and I used to associate it with old people and Radio 2. But it's really grown on me, especially in the open air – on bandstands and on the march. I'm well up for it. I've been looking forward to today.

Some twenty locations host separate competitions with more than a hundred bands from all over the country dashing in their coaches from contest to contest and competing for whatever cash prizes each community has accumulated from fund raising and donations. The event doesn't just happen: a local group or committee has devoted many hours, days and weeks to these arrangements, with planning getting underway for next year as soon as this year's bash has been put to bed. Where I now live in Lewes in East Sussex, there are no fewer than seven bonfire societies whose planning for November 5th involves hundreds of grownups and youngsters throughout the year. We have Captains of Tableaux, Set Pieces, Effigies, Torches, Aerial, Bands, Ranks, Barrels, Banners, Firesite – and an Archbishop. This is serious stuff. I would like to say that it keeps us off the streets (I'm a member of one of these societies myself) but, as anyone who has witnessed the glorious street theatre that is Lewes bonfire will know, the opposite would be true. Some of these pyromaniacs are doubtless active volunteers in some other life. For some of the teenagers involved this may be an alternative to hanging around at a loose end. The pride and vigour with which these young volunteer marshals "sort" ill-behaved interlopers on the 5th makes you glad you're on the same side.

Here in Saddleworth there may be prizes for best band, best youth band, best soloist and so on. A single, experienced assessor at each location – generally the only person being paid for their time and expertise – sits, screened from the bands in a caravan or upstairs room, and scores them as "Band 1, Band 2" etc to ensure that the competition is determined not on the basis of name or reputation, but on performance and merit on the day. Those, like me, watching in the flesh are told the name of each band by a simple sign paraded in front of us, by yet another young volunteer. Well, it's a line on your CV.

It is possible for a spectator or supporter to drive between the contests, following a favourite band, but many opt, as I'm doing, to choose a venue, park myself and wait for the bands to come to me. Friends Helen and Phil from nearby Marple, who have already put me up on this walk, have come with me to Uppermill and we are enthusiastically supporting the local beer, ice cream and hot dog economy.

Each band disembarks from its coach near the small visitor centre and marches in smart livery, playing a competition piece, different from the one they will perform on arrival at the contest site. If we stay here throughout we may see over fifty bands, but nobody is sure – the bands themselves may adjust their schedule depending on success, ambition or even the traffic.

First up for us, according to the young lady with the placard, is the Bad Ass Band. And, perhaps to make the point, they have a very tarnished looking tuba. They're followed in orderly sequence by bands from all over the country – young and not so young. Local favourites, Uppermill, earn an extra loud cheer: will that be picked up by the assessor?

This is clearly a national event but surely the gritty miners of Lancashire and Yorkshire will have the edge over the poncy southern hedge fund managers and cappuccino sippers? Except they did away with the miners some years ago to give the southern bands a chance.

Is it, I wonder, physically possible for a cornet player to hit one of those high notes without raising his eyebrows? Still they come: Hammonds Saltaire Band, Hanwell Silver Band (more southerners) and Dobcross Junior (another local village holding its own competition today).

The pensioners have obviously turned up early with their folding chairs, blankets, thermos and sandwiches for their free day out, have claimed the front row and won't be shifted for hours. We join the lurkers with the pushchairs, beer cans and dogs at the back, handily placed for the enticing waft of the catering vans and able to chat without annoying other people. That's one of the good things about brass bands, that they're not easily put off by coughs, whispers, a watch with a noisy tick or the constant call of, "Do you want onions on that?" as the Halle Orchestra might be.

I don't hear much from the audience in the way of detailed musical critique of the performance pieces, but I don't think that's the point for those watching. I recognise some of the tunes, but I can't do that "play along thing" my dad used to do with his cheeks. They're certainly not all marches; there are classical pieces, compilations from musicals, ABBA tunes, stirring ones, wistful

111

ones, and they've been selected to showcase the talents of each band and its soloist.

The rain, threatening for a while, has arrived and is getting heavier. As the afternoon heads towards evening local youngsters are on the move, warming up no doubt for one of the big nights of the social calendar. Bearing in mind the wet and the less than warm temperatures, some of the louder girls seem under-dressed.

We agree that the weather isn't likely to improve, that we've sampled the day enjoyably and have no need to stick it out into the early hours. As we head towards the car we spot some of the rock stars of the brass band scene, like Black Dyke Mills and Grimethorpe Colliery, arriving in their coaches. But by now it really is wet, and we don't stop.

We check the results next day. The "best band" award in Uppermill went to the Windcorp Band. They're Swedish.

A few weeks ago, my walk brought me from Stalybridge along the Huddersfield Canal to Uppermill and that's where I need to resume this morning. Helen drops me off with Phil close to where, yesterday, we watched the competing bands. The village is quiet and shows no sign of the previous day's activities.

We set off along the towpath and our first stop is at a small café and visitor centre at Brownhill. When I worked for Greater Manchester Council in the 1970s and 80s, we restored and converted this former canal side warehouse into a small countryside information centre for this part of the Tame Valley. Somehow our original aims of encouraging the public to explore, appreciate and enjoy the local countryside through changing exhibitions and a ranger presence have evolved into a few tired looking display panels upstairs, but it's good to see the building still open and functioning and the catering side is clearly doing good business.

A further short walk along the canal to Diggle and this time we can justify a stop at Grandpa Greene's Ice Cream Parlour and Café. "It's hand-made in Saddleworth," and probably, in terms of its creamy-looking content and taste, highly life-shortening. Still, if there aren't any actual scary numbers written on it, who cares?

It's now raining heavily again and sitting in the café's outside area wasn't such a good idea. We need to get going anyway because we have a boat to catch. Helen is due to meet up with us just along the towpath to take a trip on a narrow boat (believe me, it has to be narrow) from Diggle through the Standedge Tunnel, apparently the longest (at 5,500 yards, or over three miles) and highest tunnel on Britain's canal network. This will take us through, or under, the Pennines into Yorkshire proper.

I did plan to walk the whole route from the Irish Sea to the North Sea but told myself it was OK to make a couple of exceptions. Crossing the Mersey estuary from Birkenhead to Liverpool would have been no fun at all on foot; I anticipate Standedge Tunnel being a highlight of my trek and, with no room for a towpath, it doesn't offer a pedestrian option. I suppose I could just keep walking up and down the boat.

Construction of the tunnel took from 1794 to 1811 and was the costliest on the network. With no towpath, boats were "legged" through – one or more boatmen lay on their backs on the cargo and pushed against the roof or walls of the tunnel with their legs. Professional leggers were paid one shilling and sixpence for working a boat from one end to the other, which took three hours with a full load and about half that for an empty boat. You'd struggle to get anyone to do it for those wages now, wherever they came from.

The tunnel saw commercial working until 1921 but the canal was officially closed in 1944 after which it soon fell into disrepair. But, as we've already seen, a committed band of enthusiasts (with major support from funding agencies), campaigned and got their hands dirty for year after year until, in May 2001, the whole of the Huddersfield Narrow Canal with its iconic tunnel was reopened for navigation.

We've booked ourselves onto a covered passenger boat that runs each way through the tunnel on certain summer Saturdays, in our case west to east from Diggle to Marsden. Our vessel is *Pennine Pride*, our host is Fred. Fred has completed nearly 10,000 trips through the tunnel and claims he's rarely lost a passenger. He's had that Prince Charles through, and Michael Portillo; he clearly knows his stuff and seems unlikely to get us lost.

We get an initial briefing (no swimming, no snorkelling, no wi-fi, no duty free). Nobody expects you to stay seated inside. There's a small open area at both front and back, which is great – except where there's water coming through the roof of the tunnel.

In part brick-lined, especially where it passes beneath the near-parallel rail tunnels, much of the route is through the natural limestone. It's extremely narrow in places, with frequently no more than a foot's clearance to either side. Although a number of passing places were created, the idea of two-way working was soon abandoned – you really wouldn't want to meet anyone coming towards you. As it contains a significant S bend where the tunnellers from either end didn't quite meet (come on, this was more than 200 years ago, what were you expecting?), the "light at the end of the tunnel" can't be seen until we're past the bend – so you're basically looking into the darkness. And it's fabulous.

Fred keeps us entertained with tales of Yorkshire folk trying to escape to Lancashire through the tunnel (OK, it may have been the other way around) and people falling off boats then being run over when their other half has reversed to search for them. It's dark going backwards, you see. We get a shock when we catch sight of a ghost vehicle up a side tunnel to our right. It turns out to be our official "shadow" in a van, tracking us – a health and safety requirement.

Our trip takes around two hours and we feel very superior to the people taking the 30 minutes "taster" trip into the tunnel from the Marsden portal. At Marsden we disembark and take a look around the excellent visitor centre and drink our cups of tea while exchanging salty tales of our adventures and we pen the odd shanty to mark the occasion.

On Sunday morning, Marsden looks a bit like Happy Valley in the TV series with its stone houses and slate roofs – only without Sarah Lancashire and a psychopathic killer, and, this morning, much wetter. My first port of call today is at Marsden's Mechanics Institute; a fine, renovated building dating originally from 1861 when its grand opening was marked by a procession around the village led by the local brass band.

Mechanics' Institutes were founded as educational establishments, essentially to provide adult education (particularly in technical subjects), to working men. As such, they were often funded by local industrialists on the grounds that they would ultimately benefit from having more knowledgeable and skilled employees. Manchester's Institute became the home for the collection of trades union banners and archives that eventually grew into the People's History Museum. In Marsden, the Institute afforded not only the prospect of education and a library but also a venue for social meetings, public lectures, musical events and dances – not much different from how it operates today.

I'm at the Institute to meet a perennial and delightful feature of the English summer, the Mikron Theatre Company, whose base is here. Mikron has travelled the canal and river network since 1972 entertaining audiences: I first saw them perform in the mid-1970s in a waterside beer garden somewhere in Staffordshire and they're as fresh now as they were then. My initial understanding was that their plays were based around canals, canal boats and the people who worked and lived on them, but I suppose, over the years, the scope may have become strained and the repertoire now embraces new plays on a range of historic social and industrial subjects. This year's output comprises *Pure: the Business of Chocolate* (with a storyline embracing Quakerism, overbearing industrialists, aggressive marketing, a tight-fisted landlord and the deserving poor, over two different time periods – following so far?) and *Canary Girls: Heroes on the Home Front* (two sisters in 1914, formerly maids and now munitions workers, the dangers of shell work, chasing one's dream, union activity – and the deserving poor). Themes for next year will be the RNLI and YHA. And, one would assume, at least some deserving poor.

Every play involves music, songs and truckloads of humour. Sets are simple. They need to be to be transported around the country on *Tyseley* (the company's 80-year-old narrow boat), or by van, and assembled and dismounted speedily each day by the cast. About 450 applications are received each year for four acting roles: two male, two female. And they earn their pay, being called on to act, perform on a variety of musical instruments and hump scenery around. Despite performing against a backdrop of people eating and drinking, the delivery is strong, and I can hear every word, ensuring that the witty, pointed song lyrics are not wasted. That may seem like a pedantic artistic "critique", but that's me: if somebody's gone to the trouble of writing something funny I'd like to hear what it is…

The company's artistic director, Marianne McNamara, suggests a coffee shop along the road for a chat. As with most of the groups that I'm visiting on my walk, Mikron can presumably never feel totally confident about where their future funding will come from, but Marianne seems upbeat about the company's prospects. The company is a registered charity with its own board of trustees. Perhaps, along with all the hard work and the professionalism, it helps that Mikron has its own distinct niche in the performing world. Approximately 70% of their annual income is generated by their own direct efforts, through ticket receipts and merchandise, but they have been well supported by the "wonderful" Esmee Fairbairn Foundation, the Arts Council, special appeals and Mikron's own "Friends" group. Marianne refers to partnership arrangements with other community groups, but I surely detect a raising of the eyebrows at mention of David Cameron's (you may remember him?) "Big Society".

I ask about *Tyseley*, the iconic narrow boat at the heart of Mikron. With the company being based just a short walk from the Marsden portal of Standedge Tunnel, it was planned for *Tyseley* in 2001 to be the first boat to travel on the fully reopened Huddersfield Narrow Canal. Unfortunately, she showed her age, and some middle-age spread caused her to get stuck in a lock. (At least it's good to be thought of as middle-aged if, like *Tyseley*, you were born in 1936.)

I study the touring programme to see where I can catch Mikron when they will be performing outdoors and Tyseley based. This turns out to be at a marina south of Oxford later in the summer. As well as being an excellent production in a fine setting, this provides an opportunity for me to catch up with Marianne and her colleagues. Long may they stay afloat.

From Marsden I'm aiming for Huddersfield tonight. I'm following the Huddersfield Canal which sounds reassuring. For once the sun comes out and it's warm! There are typical Pennine sandstone houses with gardens running down to the canal. And mills. I've seen lots of those on this walk. Many are still in some form of commercial use even if it's not the original one; plenty more have been converted into highly desirable apartments. Where there seems to be less money about, mills stand empty awaiting better times.

The path is downhill – I've crossed, or at least tunnelled beneath – the Pennine chain.

Perhaps it's the sunshine but this is proving to be one of the most enjoyable stretches of the walk so far – calves in the fields, gorgeous views of Pennine farmland. It's Sunday and I have company on the towpath today: walkers, cyclists, families, young and not so young couples. With so many people about there is etiquette to be observed: how dogwalkers handle their charges when they pass other walkers like me; how they resolve any dog-to-dog issues; how cyclists behave when they want to overtake walkers, or pass them in the opposite direction; when is it appropriate for walkers to greet or even acknowledge each other – do you have to be more than a certain distance from a car park, or above a particular contour? I'm hoping someone will ask me where I've walked from or where I'm aiming for, so I can casually indicate a hundred miles or more in either direction. I don't have to tell them that it's taking me around six months...

I reach Slaithwaite and feel in need of a break. This walking thing isn't something I've done a lot of in recent years and I look forward to my breaks more than seems respectable. I pass the relatively new micro, Empire Brewery on the canal side and a busy bakery and café but I'm looking for somewhere that I won't need to stand in a queue (tiredness gets me like that) and press on to the Shoulder of Mutton in the attractive town centre to replenish my liquid level. Just beyond the pub is a bench on the towpath, where I sit and eat my butty and crisps. I spin out my stop by downloading emails on my mobile to see if there have been any special offers on Christmas hampers and decide whether to go with today's Wowcher voucher for a face mask. I really ought to work out how to cancel those, though they do make me feel wanted.

A short distance beyond Slaithwaite I reach Linthwaite and my eye is inevitably drawn to a huge mill a few hundred yards away on the bank of the River Colne, bearing the name *Titanic.*

A quick thumbing of my mobile tells me (this is definitely a useful alternative to dragging myself over to it) that the old wool mill dates from 1911 and its grand opening was celebrated – in the only conceivable way – by Linthwaite Band on a platform specially erected on top of the mill chimney. I'm reminded at this point about another musical ensemble performing on a different *Titanic* around that time and how that didn't end well...

Since 2005 the mill has accommodated an eco-spa (?) and apartments and I can inform you, courtesy of their own website, that in 2015: *Titanic Spa smashes the record for an English Spa gaining five awards in one night at The Spa Traveller Awards.*

...which, I confess, is something that I didn't pick up from *The Guardian* at the time.

This is an attractive stretch with wildflowers in the fields, oaks and sycamores along the towpath and reedmace (bulrushes) lining the canal. As usual I'm arriving in a major town by the back door but this approach to Huddersfield takes some beating with its array of restored and converted mills.

Part of the path is blocked by industrial units, diverting the route, then it's back to the towpath and university buildings, old and new. I'm definitely flagging now and am very pleased to reach today's destination, the Premier Inn – and that's not a phrase I've used often.

In truth I had been keen to book myself into Huddersfield's George Hotel in the town centre. It looks great in the photographs and has history: it's Victorian and Grade II listed and, for those like me who allocate too great a percentage of our brain to these things, it's where Rugby League was discovered. At least, it was here in August 1895 that twenty-one Lancashire and Yorkshire rugby clubs voted by 20 to 1 to "Secede from the Union" and set up their own Northern Rugby Football Union which, in 1922, became the Rugby Football League. The schism was based on the issue of "broken time" payments – the hard-bitten northerners wanted to be compensated for lost wages when playing (it's those deserving poor again); the southern toffs were no doubt content to fall back on their investment portfolios.

The British Amateur Rugby League Association (BARLA) was also founded at the George Hotel in 1973, and in 2005 the Rugby League Heritage Centre was opened in the basement. Sadly, the hotel closed in 2013 and, at the time of writing, is still awaiting a positive future.

But for now, the Premier Inn will do just fine. It looked good on the website, right on a basin of the Huddersfield Canal. I feel I ought to be out on the town, exploring, but I've got two nights here and I'm knackered. The "meal deal" at the Inn allows me to order extra ribs ("whole rack") for £1.99 so I'm incapable of movement. I'm conscious that Bill Bryson devoted what felt like 50% of his *Road to Little Dribbling* to grumbling about how the cost of sandwiches has increased over the last twenty years: tag along with me, Bill, I know where the good deals are.

It's been a good night's sleep, it has to be said. Premier Inn seem to focus much of their advertising on this point, and fair do's. There's even a choice of pillow types – and I don't even get that at home. And signs dotted around urging quiet between 10pm and 7am. Come to think of it, I don't get that at home either.

The breakfast is fine; all the hotel staff that I meet are personable. For someone like me that takes pride in a decent grumble it's a real downer.

I'm off across the town centre to catch a bus. There's a busy dual carriageway ring road between me and the Kingsgate Centre so I observe where and when the locals run across in order to give myself the best chance. I'm not sure there's another option.

The shopping centre itself is pleasant. That is, it's more or less empty which amounts to the same thing. I'm early, the cleaners are still in possession of the mall and the first of the store staff are pressing codes into keypads to raise the shutters on a new day's retailing pleasure.

Back onto the real streets, past the Lawrence Batley Theatre (where I'll be this evening), and following signs to the town's main railway station. I've seen pictures, but the reality is still overwhelming. The station has a classical façade with a portico and Corinthian columns dominating the pedestrianised St George's Square. It's Grade I listed, and the frontage was described by John Betjeman, who knew a thing or two about stations, as the most splendid in England. There are two pubs within the frontage, either side of the main entrance.

And there's a station cat! What more could you ask of a station? Felix joined the staff in 2011 and maintains a patrol to keep the place free of rodents. She (she? Felix?) has her own cat-flap to bypass the ticket barriers. She was promoted in 2016 to the position of Senior Pest Controller and has her own hi-vis jacket and name badge. My source is silent on the question of equal opportunities recruitment, the nature of any competitive interview and any TUPE issues that might arise, but I can relate that she has, at time of writing, over 87,000 followers on Facebook – which seems as good a performance indicator as any.

At one side of the square stands the George Hotel where I had hoped to lay my head amongst the ghosts of Rugby League Past. But now it's clearly not "open for business"; an expression used by politicians when they don't have actual policies on the economy. I try the doorbell at the George a few times in the hope that some kind soul might let me wander around inside, but nothing doing, so I cross the square to have a chat with Harold Wilson, born of this parish. Harold now stands eight feet tall, caught permanently in mid-stride, sans pipe and HP sauce bottle, and was unveiled by Tony Blair in Prime Minister mode in 1999.

I've still got that bus to catch at Huddersfield's main bus station and I'm queuing behind some very chatty women who clearly regard buying a ticket in the same way that I might browse in a book shop. The staff dealing with enquiries and ticket sales are really helpful and friendly – we're just not used to this in the south east. They tell me that my Sussex bus pass will give me a free trip to my destination – the National Coal Mining Museum for England – so I'm well chuffed. This is proper adventure stuff and I'm managing it without a team of researchers and porters.

I remember what to do on unfamiliar buses and I ask the driver to tell me when to get off. The bus seems busy for 10 a.m. and wanders through housing estates, the open countryside and outlying settlements. We get long views of the Emley Moor transmitter and scattered wind turbines, and of the cooling towers of two power stations in the distance. They're off to the east in the direction I'll be walking tomorrow, and seem worryingly far away. I make a note that it's warm and sunny.

We reach the stop for the museum and the driver gives me re-joining instructions.

We're at Caphouse Colliery, now home to the museum. It's a belter – full, illustrated and multi-dimensional accounts of the

1984/85 miners' strike, the Wives' Support Groups and literature, art, music, community, disasters, politics, history, domestic health, housing, hobbies, pets, allotments, galas, engineering and technology, church and chapel, whippets, pigeons, rescue, industrial relations and career patterns associated with mining and miners.

I book a trip underground. In addition to our guide, Keith, there are four others in our group – a middle-aged chap and a family group comprising a woman of thirty or so and what appear from their conversation to be her father and grandfather. I'm relieved there's not more as I don't thrive in crowded, confined spaces and have, in my time, made one or two inglorious exits from trips like this. Just don't mention the Chilean miners to me.

Keith has worked at the colliery in some capacity or other for nearly 50 years. Our tour underground lasts an hour with some tense moments for me when passages narrow and roofs lower, and I definitely don't enjoy the sound of a large school party approaching us from behind. We pass models of men, women, children and horses illustrating periods of mining history, together with impressive equipment. It's clear that we're seeing a cleaner, less cluttered, safer environment than would have been the case when the mine was being worked but nevertheless it's sobering. And Keith has some great rat stories.

After the tour there's still plenty to see around the site. The pithead baths look very chummy: a sign informs us that miners were expected to wash one another's backs. I can't see that turning out well at any job I've ever had. And there are stables complete with pit ponies. I learn that Northumberland's Ellington Colliery only ceased using ponies in 1994.

At the inevitable museum shop I'm disappointed not to see any brass band CDs – that seems like a missed opportunity – but I buy a book, *Settling Scores: the Media, the Police and the Miners'*

Strike as I feel in that sort of mood after my visit. After the long overdue Hillsborough reckoning it looks like the truth about the 1984 Battle of Orgreave might eventually be revealed.

I'm an incurable leaflet gatherer and pick up one that's advertising a performance at the museum of a stage version of the 1996 film *Brassed Off*, about the effects of pit closures on a northern mining community and its brass band. The film starred Tara Fitzgerald, and probably some other people. But mainly Tara Fitzgerald. In one scene, the fictitious Grimley Colliery band, with the eponymous colliery about to close and its members put out of work, drink more than is strictly appropriate for an outfit competing at the Saddleworth Whit Friday gathering. SPOILER ALERT: the band recovers from this low point to achieve national fame at the Albert Hall, where band conductor Pete Postlethwaite gets to utter the immortal line: "I used to think that music mattered. But does it? Bollocks! Not compared to how people matter." (A line borrowed, as fans of Chumbawamba may recognise, for the intro to their hit *Tubthumping* – which may come in handy for quiz purposes.) And, did I mention, Tara Fitzgerald is really good in the film?

Brassed Off, the play, will feature the City of Bradford Brass. The coal mining museum would be a brilliant place to see the play, even without Tara Fitzgerald, but the dates just don't work out for me.

But now I have the smell of brass in my nostrils and search the web for sightings of the play. I find one scheduled in the next week or two in East Grinstead, a seething centre of political agitation, working class struggle and anti-Thatcherism near my home in Sussex. (I believe I'm using what is called irony.) When I'm next home, I buy myself a ticket and head to the theatre to be met in the foyer by several young members of the cast chanting and waving placards, much to the obvious dismay of one or two of the good citizens of East Grinstead who are as likely to agree to shout, "The Workers United Will Never be Defeated!" as eat their own liver. I suspect that those who remember the film only as comedy will have been in for a surprise. A woman two seats away from me puts her fingers firmly into her ears whenever the band plays, which suggests she may have come to the wrong play.

I'm not going to pretend that my bus journey from the museum back to Huddersfield is particularly enthralling but there is, for me, one unusual element – which explains the "re-joining" instructions given by my bus driver this morning. There is a bus stop on one side of the road only, alongside a pub car park. I don't think this is penny pinching: it's because the other side has no pavement, just a tall hedge, and sight lines over there are rubbish. So, I've been told to wait by the pub until I see the bus approaching on the far side of the road, wave at it, then run across in front of it, hoping all the while that the driver has seen me and intends to stop. How all this works out at night I'm not sure. I suppose this is quite normal in the countryside but to a townie it's jolly exciting.

There's a strong smell from the fields of rape as we pass by. A light rain starts to fall which becomes torrential by the time I get off the bus not far from my hotel. As I carry all my luggage for the week on my back, I'm not blessed with many changes of clothing and I'm struggling to work out how, having now drenched roughly half of my kit in a dash from the bus, I can get to the theatre and back tonight in this continuing downpour and still have something wearable to walk in tomorrow. I discover that there is in fact an answer to this little conundrum: I just get wet and stay wet. Simple.

I spend the evening dripping messily at the Lawrence Batley Theatre. Originating in 1819 as a Methodist chapel, the building has experienced a number of incarnations and was eventually rescued and restored to life by the Kirklees Theatre Trust around twenty years ago in its present form. It's a lovely venue. Tonight's offering is *Fewer Emergencies*. There is no admission price; we're invited to pay what we feel appropriate when we leave, which seems a tad risky to me.

I read the programme in the bar before the performance begins. It contains words that I really don't want to see there, like *challenging, thought provoking* and *contemporary* (which gets three mentions). And, especially, *biomechanics*. And *project*. I think I'd have preferred a nice musical.

We're invited to go through from the bar to the space where the action will presumably take place. Chairs are set out in two rows around three sides of the room and we sit in silence for several minutes. It may be a while before I eat anything and there's a small pack of emergency custard creams in the pocket of my anorak. As frequently happens these days, I find it ridiculously hard to open so I start jabbing at it with the end of my pedometer, which is the only vaguely tool-like object I have on me. This is the first time I discover that it has a personal alarm function, possibly handy for future reference but definitely ill-timed.

The cast is made up of four quite young women who may be from round these parts and a white haired Scottish bloke who may be the ringleader. There are around 40 to 50 in the audience and I'm feeling anxious that I'm sat in the front – there's no stage – when an actor (if that's the right word), advances and points at me while maintaining eye contact throughout. I'm mentally knocking pounds off my voluntary donation.

There are three 20 minute "plays". In the first one, a young woman marries the bloke and there are repercussions through her life, I think. In the second one the bloke shoots a receptionist somewhere then shoots kids in a school – perhaps the receptionist is at the school too – and they end up singing about a postman. The third one, I have no idea – I think three people may have died but I don't know who they are.

They say you should be prepared to try anything once, except folk music and incest. I'm beginning to think there may be other candidates.

After the three performances, there's a drinks and loo break and we're expected back to discuss the plays with the cast and director. I don't think so.

But, hey, it's almost stopped raining as I slosh back to the hotel for supper, where I have a nice chat with the receptionist (not the one who got shot). She can read me like a book and tells me when there will be a ukulele band coming to perform here at the canal basin, where I can see a chap who makes balloon dogs while skateboarding, hitting himself on the head with a tin tray and singing *Ghost Riders in the Sky*, and where I can get my beard into Huddersfield's very own ice cream. But I think she made one of those up.

It's misty this morning over the canal but soon clears to a watery sunshine. I'll be walking to Dewsbury today where I'm booked on a train homewards late afternoon. Over breakfast, I'm reading a piece in the *Huddersfield Examiner*, 'Twelve reasons you should never go to Dewsbury.' Well, I've never been but I feel committed now. But it turns out to be something of a puff piece for the place – pictures of wildlife, sunset, arts and culture festival.

I set off along the canal with a spring in my step, or as close as I get. The path is lined with hawthorn in blossom and there is healthy plant life in and out of the water. Sunlight breaks through the trees and the vegetation is reflected in the surface of the canal.

In the kind of crime thrillers that I watch on TV it seems a given that an early morning walk or jog along a canal towpath should guarantee a sighting of at least one waterlogged corpse but happily today is clearly an exception. I hear birdsong and regret having no idea what it's coming from. There's a mummy duck with eight little ones, but I'm pretty sure that's not the source of the song. I pass a church converted into a house, then a council waste recycling site on the far bank. It's quite an industrial scene but it's noticeably green as well, and I don't see any litter or rubbish in the water or on the path.

I'm following instructions from last night's hotel receptionist to find Dixons ice cream shop. Shop? Is that what they're called? Parlour? It's a very short detour from the towpath and faces right onto the busy A62 Leeds Road. That feels like a strange location until you notice the modern John Smith's stadium nearby, formerly known by various other sponsors' names, and home to both Huddersfield Town Football Club and Huddersfield Giants Rugby League team. And there's an out of town cinema and a trading estate. The ice cream lady, Julie, tells me they queue round the block at lunch times and on match days but this morning I have the place to myself. It's been open since 8 a.m. but this isn't my usual time for a cone or a nice wafer, especially just after a hotel "full English".

But I'm here in the interests of research. Dixons is a family firm, making their traditional ice cream since 1961 from locally sourced milk without the usual additives – so you can make your beard messy and feel that you're doing your bit for the planet at the same time. And plenty of people clearly do: I see that TripAdvisor ranks Dixons' other branch in Huddersfield as number 1 of 497 places to eat in the town (the second outlet that I'm in is really a takeaway only).

I ask for a small vanilla tub, but Julie points out that the white stuff that I can see doesn't contain vanilla, just milk. And it's delicious.

Julie tells me how they train the shop/parlour assistants to be welcoming, to remember that it's nice that people actually want to eat their ice cream. I can't see that catching on, especially in the British catering industry. We chat about walking – it's still quiet in the shop – and Julie's plans to walk the Wainwright coast to coast route with her husband, which she thinks might be more scenic than the way I'm doing it.

Back onto the towpath. This is Huddersfield Broad Canal, distinguishing it from the Narrow Canal that I'd been following as far as Huddersfield. And it's the same size. Except for the locks: they're broader, and it's the width of the locks that determines the size of the boats that can pass through.

I'm passing a few people today: walkers, cyclists, people listening to music through headphones, and quite an ethnic mix. A chap with a dog wants to know where I'm heading and recommends a route. This is helpful: for once I need to forsake the comfort of a clear-cut route along the towpath and cut across to join the River Calder flowing towards Dewsbury.

This link is a complicated one and I'm making frequent use of my OS map. I try to climb up onto an aqueduct to carry me across the river Colne but that's fenced off, so back to the towpath which I eventually leave at a busy B road. This climbs steeply after crossing the river and I'm puffing heavily when I join part of the National Cycle Network route 66. A chap on a bike who looks older than me (or so I tell myself) calls a friendly greeting but I'm in no fit state and ignore him – I live in the south now, where it's expected. We don't say hello to anyone when out walking unless we're above 1,000 feet.

I'm all in favour of the NCN: part of my job when I worked for East Sussex County Council was to help plan the routes through the county. It's a tougher job than you might think – not every village or residential street or landowner or motorist, walker or horse rider wants to see you succeed. I secured a small award from the Winston Churchill Memorial Trust to visit Denmark and the Netherlands for a month to see how they overcame any obstacles and built such impressive cycle networks. I enjoyed the experience but I'm not sure that it helped much in my day job. In Sussex, we start from a low baseline of cycling activity, especially outside the main towns, and could spend a fortune changing road layouts and creating off-road tracks without making much difference. Our councillors were more readily influenced by hostile landowners and motorists and the task was an uphill struggle. Cycling seems to be on the increase generally now, which must be a good thing environmentally and health wise, and it's encouraging to see facilities improving in London and elsewhere. But East Sussex, outside of Brighton or Hastings? Hmm.

I stick with NCN 66 until I have a choice of route and I opt to re-join the riverbank at Battyeford Cut Bridge where I come across three boats marked 'Safe Anchor Charitable Trust'. Some of the youngsters aboard appear noticeably challenged and are being supported and cared for, and I can see references to the Duke of York's Community Initiative. Waterways clearly have a role to play in social welfare: the Wooden Canal Boat Society that I met in Ashton under Lyne run their Wellbeing trips and I'm due to meet a charitable project called Sobriety at the Yorkshire Waterways Museum when I reach Goole.

At Mirfield I'm confused, which happens with increasing frequency I find. My towpath has run out, there's both a river and a canal, as well as NCN 66 again. Even with my trusty map I don't know where I'm going, and I'm tired, which makes any false call into a minor disaster. But heroically I pull through somehow and re-join the canal towpath.

The canal is broad here and rich with may blossom and bird-song. At Shepley Bridge Marina there are Variety Club vans and a mini-coach which I associate with volunteers and days out for ill, disabled and disadvantaged children. Not for the first time on this walk I feel humbled by the essential decency I'm encountering.

The canal joins the River Calder, lined with oak, alder, birch and poplar. Across the river there are anglers angling on an extensive pond, and swans with downy cygnets. And there's a distinctive, almost sweet smell which I can identify from my early career in the environmental field – some may have a nose for the wild garlic, for me it's landfill. I don't know from what combination of rancid and putrescent decaying domestic waste it's distilled but I'd recognise it anywhere. One of my first jobs involved locating and visiting nearly 70 old tips that the newly formed Greater Manchester Council had inherited from its predecessor councils with a view to developing a programme for closing them and converting them into woods and parkland. They gave me a card to carry round in my wallet which, I was informed, would protect me from catching something called Weil's disease which I would otherwise undoubtedly contract from rat's urine with consequential organ failure and death. I hope there was more to my health and safety protection than that, but I suspect not.

I reach the entrance to the Calder and Hebble Navigation Canal and this might have been my chosen route eastwards had I not been drawn by the bright lights (OK, the station) of Dewsbury. I climb up to a disused railway line (NCN 66 again) to cross the River Calder then turn back to the river bank past engineering workshops and a building storing bedheads and past two women joggers, a cyclist and – memorably – a man riding two horses. This is NCN 69, Spen Valley Way, which picks up the line of yet another former railway into the heart of Dewsbury.

I only know Dewsbury from school geography: you know the sort of thing – Manchester famed for cotton, Sheffield for cutlery, Dewsbury for shoddy and mungo. They're types of cloth based on fibres recycled from woollen rags. My overwhelming impression, apart from the fact that the station seems to be at the top of a hill and I'm whacked, is of a hugely impressive array of late 19th/early 20th century municipal and commercial buildings. This, it's clear, is the heart of Dewsbury Conservation Area. What wealth, what civic pride. So rich in heritage, but so clearly poor in maintenance. I'm standing next to swimming baths that are, at a guess, Edwardian, with first and second class entrances clearly labelled and, from more modern signage, may be in part occupied by a squash club and a night club. So many of these fine buildings appear to be unused, possibly derelict, while others, if occupied at all, sport inappropriate shop fronts and signs. One can but hope that wealth returns to Dewsbury while there's still the opportunity to save this fine heritage.

I've arrived early at the station and ask at the ticket office how much it would cost me to switch to an earlier train south. It's either a two and a half hour wait or pay another £65. I guess I've always wanted to spend more time in Dewsbury.

Chapter 7

Cats, Bats, Liquorice and Early Baths

It's early July. It's taken me over a month to return to Dewsbury but that's not the fault of the train service. Life sometimes intervenes in one's travel plans.

I phone for a taxi to take me from the station to the finest hotel accommodation I have ever visited in Britain or elsewhere. The taxi driver hasn't heard of it and can't locate the address given on the website; the same applies to his "control". I bring up Google Maps on my mobile and we eventually find ourselves bumping down a long, steep, unmade, unsigned track to be confronted by big metal gates and an intercom. I know I must be in the right place because I recognise the hotel logo and the staff members' purple livery from the website. I feel out of my league here, yet I know I could afford to stay. It's just that I know they won't have me; I don't meet their specification, not being a cat.

The Ings Luxury Cat Hotel is simply a knockout. Set up, owned and managed by a lovely Yorkshire couple who had been reluctant to leave their own pets in catteries or kennels when they went away on holiday, the Ings now provides 5-star luxury with twelve suites (yes, suites) in the spa building and six more in the lodge for "activity holidays" (climbing equipment, steps, lookout posts inside and out) and 100% occupancy throughout the year. Jo and Phil have developed a very distinctive business model which the Ritz can only envy.

- ☐ Beautifully appointed, decorated and colour themed accommodation – tick (even Jo's eyeshadow matches the décor)
- ☐ Four poster beds – tick
- ☐ A welcome tray with the guest's own name on it, bearing shrimp delights and other tasty nibbles – tick
- ☐ Large flat screen TVs showing alluring visions of denizens of the deep – tick
- ☐ Afternoon tea served in the comfort of your own suite – tick
- ☐ Bedtime stories and birthday celebrations – tick
- ☐ Weekly disco with disco lights and prizes – tick
- ☐ Personalised (felicised?) party bag on departure – tick
- ☐ Skype for feline guest and human "significant other" – tick
- ☐ Individual wee/poo chart – tick

After my own conducted tour – and afternoon tea (though not served in my own, named bowl) – I walk outside with Phil to admire the grounds and the fine view over much of West Yorkshire, taking in the rugby league grounds of Huddersfield, Batley, Dewsbury and Wakefield. Phil tells me that both he and Jo are locals and moved to this house about a dozen years ago. Jo was mad about cats, Phil more of a dog person, so a cattery it became! He mentioned "planning issues" (being in the green belt), but relative isolation from neighbours was a plus point. (Sometimes I just don't get around to mentioning my day job as a planner...).

Jo, it seems, is the trigger for new ideas – from the homegrown catnip and immaculate, hi-tech litter trays to the mayoral opening with entertainers. I ask if there are plans for further expansion, perhaps for franchising the concept. It seems not: the *status quo,* it appears, provides a good work/life balance for the family (son, daughter and father are all involved) and it's Jo's personal touch that makes the whole thing fly.

As if responsibility for the nation's most spectacular cat hotel were not enough, I learn that Phil has another entry in the *Hall of Quirky Fame*, as a former winner of the annual coal sack carrying race in the local village of Gawthorpe. The course is nearly a mile. I ask about technique; Phil replies, "Don't stop," which seems fair enough. Globalisation has impacted even here, and entries come from around the world. I'm wondering whether those people in Finland who do that wife carrying race start with an advantage. I'm also wondering – since the local collieries have all closed – where the coal comes from... Oh, surely not.

Phil kindly gives me a lift to my hotel along the Wakefield Road, which will put me in the right direction for tomorrow. It's a small, family run, friendly place. I dine in, then fall asleep on my bed in front of the telly watching re-runs of *QI*.

It's raining in the morning when I wake but the TV weatherman says it'll improve, so I stir myself and manage yet again to tackle the full English. This is what I'm like when my wife isn't around.

The morning is still grey and damp when I set out towards the River Calder, past Earlsheaton cemetery with its impressive Victorian monuments and Commonwealth War Graves. But this is as close as I'm getting as the gates are firmly locked. My route takes me through residential streets and mixed commercial areas, with occasional Union Jack or St George flags on display. I don't find this uplifting. I know these things often appear in connection with sporting or other events but, as we've just experienced the EU referendum, they seem to tell a story that I'd rather not hear. My feelings towards the flag waving element of my homeland are at rock bottom.

I pass a street called Craig-y-Don, which doesn't sound Yorkshire to me, then follow Headland Lane, lined with fine stone houses on both sides, towards the river. I reach the line of an old railway and turn down it – but not before taking in a fine view of Dewsbury and its surrounds behind me to the west, a panorama of stone buildings, new industrial sheds, church towers and green hills. This is West Yorkshire. Farmland in the foreground, a train in the distance and, running through the lot are the River Calder, and the Calder and Hebble Navigation Canal – unseen from this vantage point but vital in its day and offering prospects of regeneration.

I follow the disused railway down into the valley. This is an attractive bit of countryside mingled in with settlements. A horse runs up to me. This reminds me very much of the river valleys around Manchester where I used to work. We're not talking extensive moorlands here or high peaks but important open breaks – green wedges, green lungs, call them what you will – between towns, where you might be within a few hundred yards of a main road or an old factory, or even a sewage works, but you can walk the dog, or cycle, spot a butterfly or hear a skylark. My map tells me that my route is now along Kirklees Way, which means it should be well-signed, well maintained and easy to follow. Great stuff.

I've just felt the first spots of rain. I hope it's not going to turn into anything – there's nothing like rain for buggering up your maps and your notes. And on this walk, I should know.

At the bottom of a field, I reach a stile, cross a small footbridge over a stream, then turn along a field boundary squeezed between an electric fence separating me from a field of grazing horses, and very overgrown streamside vegetation of nettles and brambles. Today is the first time on my whole walk when I've worn shorts and I'm in trouble. I really need to stop and change into something more protective, but I can't bring myself to go back and, if I try to change where I am, I'll be dropping both my rucksack and my shorts in deep black mud. I press on for a few hundred yards of purgatory. I understand the resource pressures facing councils like Kirklees but hey, if you can't do a bit better with something called Kirklees Way, it's a poor do.

I emerge from my nettles-from-hell at the site of the former Earlsheaton station and join the much better maintained Dewsbury to Ossett Greenway, or cycle route 699. This may be nature's way of telling me to entrust myself to cycle routes rather than the footpath options in this neck of the woods. I decide to stick with the greenway to Ossett as far as possible before seeking a suitable footpath to the river bank. For a drizzly day, the greenway is quite busy with dog walkers, dogs, walkers and cyclists, mainly of my age. (The dogs may have been younger.) The route climbs, bends first left, then right onto yet another old rail line towards Ossett. What were they thinking of, those railway builders? Just how many disused lines does one moderately sized Yorkshire town need? This promising route runs out where houses have been built across the line, so I look for minor roads and paths down to the river through farmland and reach a huge modern unit, Kerry Foods of Ossett. From here my path through the edge of town is narrow and overgrown, running for a mile alongside disused rail sidings – well, it makes a change.

Then along a B road to cross over a (live!) railway and there's by far the second longest train I have ever seen in the flesh, so to speak. It is attractively liveried in blue and bears the label "Drax: Powering Tomorrow: Carrying Sustainable Biomass for Cost Effective Renewable Power". I don't suppose they labelled the trains when they were just carrying boring old coal to the power station, unless it said "Coal: Like it or Lump it".

I pick up a footpath that passes through a scrapyard and onto the river bank, the first part of which means walking on bouncy planks laid into the thick mud. Eventually it emerges into more open countryside, following the grand sweeps of the River Calder, the path overgrown in places with bracken and impressive stands of Himalayan Balsam reaching ten feet in height.

I stop to eat a healthy apple and sultana "lite" cereal bar surreptitiously slipped into my rucksack by Mrs. A, and notice a blue plaque informing me this is Charles Roberts Office Park, the site of a major rail waggon building company before, you know, they closed all the railway lines. Then another cycle path under a railway bridge and the M1 motorway, still following the river, and onto a busy A road into the centre of Wakefield past light industrial units, retail parks and "leisure parks" (like retail parks but with a cinema). The bog-standard chain eateries in these "parks" all seem to be prospering but the place called Fresh Revolution that I passed on my way into town, with an image of Che Guevara in a chef's hat, offering "real affordable food for the overworked and underpaid" seems to have closed. I'm sure there's a message in that somewhere, and it's a depressing one.

I check into my hotel in the centre of Wakefield and go for a wander. As the shops and offices close for the evening the centre goes quiet. There's an impressive town hall and cathedral (both Grade I listed) and, as in Dewsbury, a fine array of Victorian stone buildings from an era when councillors and aldermen (alderpeople?) acknowledged responsibilities beyond simply keeping the council tax down. Directly opposite the Theatre Royal is Unity Hall; originally the home of Wakefield's Industrial Co-operative Society, one-time venue for silent movies and ballroom dancing, and later on for bands like the Specials, Boomtown Rats, Human League, Iron Maiden, Eurythmics and Def Leppard – and the Pretenders' first ever gig. Having gone through the cycle of decline, abandonment, dereliction and rebirth, Unity Hall is once again at the heart of the community as a centre for the arts, conferences and exhibitions. It's down to the great effort of individuals and voluntary organisations – no doubt with support from councils and businesses and funding from lottery and other sources – that places like Unity Hall survive into this century, serving new uses while providing vital links to our local heritage.

I've booked for tonight's show at the Theatre Royal. It's a lovely building inside as well as out – all wood, glass, decorated ceiling and historic light fittings – which is why I'm here, and it's been through its own cycle from theatre to cinema to bingo hall and back to theatre. It has a capacity of around 500 but I estimate it to be about one-third full this Friday evening to see *Batboy the Musical*. As there's clearly going to be plenty of space and I can see that the man in the seat next to mine is, how shall I put it, overflowing, I ask the friendly usherette if it will be in order for me to find another seat. Her response is to "ush" me to the unoccupied private box of the theatre's generous patron, which strikes me as pretty good customer care.

Batboy – not as familiar to me as, say, *Oliver!* or *West Side Story* – proves to be great fun and is almost certainly my first chiropter-an-themed musical. It majors on interspecies carnal relationships, uxoricide, filicide, and a lynch mob triggered by a Christian revivalist meeting – what's not to enjoy? It's certainly going down well with the kids, as you'd expect from that description, but the loudness of much of the music means that singers are obliged to shout throughout the songs in a variety of American accents, so some of the subtlety may be passing me by. But the audience are whooping and cheering enthusiastically which suggests that the community is refreshingly supportive of its own theatre.

And a 50 yard walk back to my hotel afterwards beats going to the West End.

*

I'm feeling guilty over breakfast. I still go for the full English but I'm taking smaller portions. And I have cereal first, which mitigates, doesn't it? I suffer a wardrobe malfunction when a rasher of bacon ends up in my lap which means I'm right out of respectable trouser wear for the rest of the week. Rain is forecast.

By taxi this morning to Nostell, a National Trust house in the Palladian style at the heart of a fine estate and parkland about six miles south east.

Visiting posh houses was what we did when I was little, along with castles and ruined abbeys. Seeing where the monks sat in a line to move their bowels was great if you were a kid but I'm afraid I never really got into all that furniture and porcelain. And you always saw it from behind a rope – no fun at all. In later years, I didn't take my own family to National Trust places very often as we had a dog that needed a lot of exercise, so we spent any free time at weekends meeting her needs – and she wasn't really into porcelain in a big way either. Only when the old Labrador died, and our day jobs tapered down a bit, did we get around to joining the Trust as members: this is what I guess the marketing people would call the "dead dog" market segment.

Two "fascinating facts" from the Trust's website which I'm happy to share. Over 43% of the rainwater in England and Wales drains through a NT property, but fortunately not always the same one. And gravity was invented by Isaac Newton in Woolsthorpe, Lincolnshire in 1665 on what is now NT land.

Never one for half measures, as soon as I became a member of the Trust, I signed up with them as a volunteer, of whom they had over 60,000 not counting me, contributing no less than 3.1 million hours of work each year. I didn't see myself as a room volunteer, lurking in a dark corner before leaping out to threaten small children, nor a conservation volunteer, setting about fence posts with a hammer or exterminating immigrant vegetation – that wouldn't do either me or the Trust any good. No, I put myself forward to serve on a committee on the grounds that you can never have enough committee meetings. I'm not sure what I contribute but I enjoy it and I'm impressed with what the organisation gets up to. In particular, I'm pleased to see that my recollection of old houses of the rich being saved for the nearly rich to savour is no longer the be all and end all of the Trust's mission.

The name of Octavia Hill comes up on a regular basis as one of the Trust's founders back in 1895. (Not enough people are christened Octavia these days, if you ask me.) As concise tributes go, it would be difficult to improve on these words from the website of her birthplace museum in Wisbech: "Octavia Hill (1838-1912) was a woman ahead of her time. An artist and a radical, she was a pioneer of affordable housing and can be seen as the founder of modern social work." Which isn't a bad way to be remembered.

This was not a woman, I'm inclined to think, who would have wanted me to peer at boring old porcelain from long range as some form of punishment for not eating up my peas at Sunday lunch. This was someone who clearly wanted me to have a good time, climbing trees, poking about in Victorian kitchens and dressing up as an undertaker's mute. Now that's worth conserving stuff for.

The Act that gave the Trust its legal standing not only stressed the importance of permanent preservation and beauty but included the phrase "for the benefit of the nation". When Fiona Reynolds took on the job of the Trust's Director General in 2000, she felt that the Trust's traditional protective approach would put people off, that in her words *(The Fight for Beauty: Our Path to a Better Future 2016)*, "I wanted people to feel involved, enthralled and engaged in the spirit of the place, and not be simply passive observers… the prevalent 'do not touch', 'do not sit here' and 'do not walk on the grass' signs had, I believed, gone beyond what was necessary for high conservation standards and risked alienating people."

There may well be Trust properties where room volunteers still like to keep visitors on a tight rein, and justifiably so, but it seems that the overall tenor is towards encouraging engagement, bringing conservation and beauty to the people and sustainably sourced cream teas to the masses. My National Trust magazine has listings of concerts, chocolate egg hunts, craft weekends, tours with the gardener, candlelight storytelling, stargazing nights and nest box building – events and activities aimed at people of all ages. But the organisation knows that its properties and programmes appeal more to audiences that are white, middle-aged to elderly and better off (a description which would also apply to the majority of its volunteers) and the Trust is keen to do more to tackle whatever barriers are working against participation by ethnic minorities, younger people and those with lower incomes. This will be a priority for the Trust over the next few years.

Conscious that, in London in particular, it owns few properties and may seem a largely irrelevant organisation to a transient population, the Trust has taken a lead recently in organising events like London Open Garden Squares Weekend, guided tours of some of the best of Britain's Brutalist concrete buildings including the Southbank Centre in London…and opening up the Big Brother house. Homosexuality was being marked by the Trust through a programme of "Prejudice and Pride" events, talks, displays and articles recognising the unconventional lifestyles witnessed by some of its properties, whether well-known figures like Vita Sackville-West, Virginia Woolf, William Banks and Oliver Messel or servants, gardeners and chauffeurs.

2018 marks the centenary of the passing of legislation granting voting rights to (some) women, following the major struggle that we've glimpsed in a previous chapter. Reading and re-reading the accounts of that fight takes you to a darker past that seems so much more than 100 years ago. Tales of heroism and extraordinary perseverance abound but my attention is caught by black humour: as a former resident of Birkenhead myself, the gathering of women at one house in that town on census night in April 1911 (part of the "No vote, No census" campaign) who completed their census return by filling in the name of a manservant on the premises and then writing, "No other persons, but many women."

The National Trust will mark the centenary of the legislation with Women and Power, a programme of events, interpretation and art projects at their properties across the country. Women closely associated with places now in the care of the Trust were prominent in both the suffrage and anti-suffrage causes. We read that Octavia Hill, co-founder of the Trust, positioned herself in the latter camp, writing in a 1910 letter to The Times, "a serious loss to our country would arise if women entered… political life". She worried that the vote would take women away from "the quiet paths of helpful, real work …". Hmm.

The Trust – to my undying gratitude – played a major role in opposing government plans to "loosen up" the planning system in order to make it easier to build houses wherever developers thought they could make a profit. This is not an organisation occupied only with the past.

I'm visiting Nostell, not just to look around a place I've not seen before, but to meet Jenny Layfield, General Manager at the property, to find how this evolution is working in practice. Not for the first time on this walk, it's pouring, and we sit in the courtyard under a large fixed umbrella as a significant contribution to the Trust's 43% share of the country's rainfall cascades around us and into our sugar basin.

Jenny came to work for the Trust as a Human Resources Adviser 12 years ago, fell in love with the organisation and has been General Manager at Nostell for the last two. One of the current imperatives across the organisation is that each property should have its own "spirit of place statement", drawn up by staff and volunteers and reflecting what's specific to the property: this will then guide future plans and decisions. At Nostell, this includes its nationally significant Robert Adam interiors, its Chippendale furniture, its works of art and dolls' house – which are conserved, displayed and brought to life through a varied programme of events and activities for the whole community throughout the year. I particularly enjoy the Trust's *50 things to do before you're 11 ¾* and *How to clean an 18th century tongue scraper.*

She mentions co-operation with other local attractions like the Yorkshire Sculpture Park, Hepworth Wakefield, the Theatre Royal and the National Coal Mining Museum, working together to promote and support one another and co-ordinate activities: collaboration with local campaigners over HS2 (or High Speed 2, the proposed rail route to reduce journey times between London and the north); the park run with 200 to 300 taking part each week through the grounds. Nostell, it seems, is in good hands.

I'm booked onto a guided tour of the house. There are two Trust volunteers and six visitors besides me. Not for the first time I'm struck by how miserable most old portrait paintings are, and how ugly the children. How did these awful people breed? Poorer glasses? Dimmer candles?

After lunch in the Nostell tearoom, I return to my walk, passing Jenny Layfield, General Manager, waiting on the main drive to welcome a wedding party. All in the job description…

I turn onto National Cycle Route 67, signed, "Wonders of Wakefield Cycle Route", through woodland, under a railway and over the River Calder to reach the Aire and Calder canal. It's pleasant, easy walking past moored commercial boats and a line of narrow boats named *Great Escape, Mrs. B and Me, C'est la Vie, Peace of Mind, Lazy Dayz* – I'm beginning to spot a theme – and Avdunnah. Avdunnah??

At Stanley Ferry there's a smart modern pub, a marina, a boatyard and an aqueduct that carries the canal over the river. There are fifty geese in a field and I can tell they're not Canadas – I'm getting good at this. And I'm being eaten by midges. Those weren't around during the earlier stages of my walk.

I'm due to meet up this afternoon with Pete, one of my oldest friends and my best man back in the day when our hair still grew in the right places. Pete has driven over from Stockport and checked into the hotel in Castleford where I have a booking for the next two nights. His plan is to walk towards me along my intended route until we meet, then escort me back to Castleford through the last couple of hours of my usual late afternoon decline. The assumption is, that if we both stick to the canal towpath, it should be hard to miss each other. The consequences of passing each other by on alternative paths are too dire to contemplate, especially as Pete is wedded to the idea that mobile phones are only for posers.

Happily, we manage a sentimental reunion directly under the M62 and we continue on our way along the Aire and Calder Navigation. Pete doesn't offer to carry my rucksack. Or me.

We pass Wakefield Europort, which seems an interesting concept marked on the map. It's hidden from view behind a high fence so I'm guessing it's a piece of ambitious labelling for a trading estate. I reach a lock connecting the canal back into the River Calder, at which point my human guide strongly advises against following the river into Castleford. He's done that once in the opposite direction, describes the horrors of the path and may resign if

I insist. We opt for an alternative following the edge of a golf course, across a live railway, through a wheat field (Pete knows this stuff), under a disused railway, past horse paddocks (clearly created across the right of way), through a farmyard, across a main road, back to the river bank and past the Calder's junction with the River Aire into Castleford. I'm indebted to John Sergeant's *Barging Round Britain* for the information that this confluence led to a local rhyme: *That's why the Castleford girls are so fair, / They bathe in the Calder and dry in the Aire.*

We pass a new "millennium" footbridge over the Aire and "the world's largest stone ground flour mill" (Allinson), and arrive at our small hotel, the Wheldale, directly opposite the town's rugby league ground.

Pete has been issuing warnings to the effect that, when he checked in at the Wheldale earlier, the bar looked decidedly "under construction" and he fears we won't get any kind of liquid refreshment on arrival. This turns out to be a false alarm for reasons that become clear later and we are both grateful. The bar area may look basic, but the landlord is very friendly, and the rooms are immaculate – and mine has the best view in the house of the Mend a Hose Jungle opposite, which is why we're here.

It's already early evening, so we limp into town to eat. Only a few yards from our hotel is a sadly boarded up pub labelled *Early Bath*, as in, "You're red carded, take an early bath," and a sign tells us it was the home of the Lock Lane Amateur Rugby League Social Club. Beautifully tiled but boarded up pubs seem to be the order of the day in Castleford, but we find the Junction open and busy, and it's a belter. Then, in traditional Saturday evening mode, it's on to the Joy Bangla for an excellent curry, and we're both glad not to be sharing a room.

*

I have timed my stay in Castleford to coincide with the annual liquorice festival in neighbouring Pontefract. This proves not to be Pete's cup of tea (liquorice seems to trigger a similar response to Marmite) so, after dropping me as near to the action as he's prepared to go, he heads home across the Pennines and leaves me to it...

...to wander along Liquorice Way, past the Haribo factory outlet (Pontefract cakes, of course) and the Liquorice Bush pub to join the throng (and I mean throng) mainlining on liquorice and blueberry ice cream (I bought some), liquorice and blueberry jam (bought some to take home), liquorice BBQ sauce on roast pork (next time), liquorice and pork pie (I ate three), liquorice and banana loaf, liquorice lads' stout – I think you get the picture. If it can be made from liquorice, decorated with liquorice or presumably if you can make it into liquorice, it's there. The stilt walkers are thinly disguised as Liquorice Allsorts. If you have never danced in the street with a nine-foot-tall woman dressed as one of those round blue jobs with little bits of something on the outside, well then, you haven't. And I'm pleased to see that the National Trust and Nostell have a stall, no doubt staffed by volunteers. You can have your face painted as...well, you can probably guess by now.

I find my way to the library to hear an illustrated talk on Greek pottery. Only kidding, it's "as seen on TV" Tom Dixon relating stories about his "life in a liquorice factory".

The sacred bush came to this country from Spain with monks and was grown successfully here because of the great depth of the soil. Our liquorice now comes from Iraq and Iran, which suggests we should be devoting our attention to the thorny question of "liquorice security" before we are threatened with rationing.

There are around 50 of us in the audience, mainly of a certain age. We're well up for Tom's personal, and occasionally saucy, liquorice-based reminiscences about *Moonraker* (the cable car cable that Jaws bites into – Pontefract liquorice), the boot that Charlie Chaplin eats in *The Gold Rush* – Pontefract liquorice), Acker Bilk miming to *Strangers on the Shore* on *Sunday Night at the London Palladium* (saxophone made of Pontefract liquorice), and John Profumo touring the liquorice factory with Christine Keeler and Mandy Rice-Davies (he would, wouldn't he?).

Tom's uncle, we are told (the last person to grow liquorice commercially in the UK), dug liquorice trenches for a living and was therefore a wow in WW1.

I'm not sure Tom's right when he claims that liquorice pipes will be reintroduced "now we're out of the EU" but I'm not going to quibble. I buy Tom's booklet of the talk, *The Sweet Fifties,* which contains the John Betjeman poem, *The Licorice Fields of Pontefract* written for Tom's aunty, the wife of the Last Grower. And on my way out of the library en route to another liquorice and pork pie, I'm heartened to see how busy the library is, and how many youngsters there are amongst the books. Perhaps they're made of... no, surely not.

But I have another commitment today and it's taking place within 20 yards of my bedroom at the hotel in Castleford.

Before today I've only been to one rugby league game, a cup final at Wembley between Barrow and Featherstone in 1967. My main memory is that the fans actually sang the national anthem in the days when football supporters didn't bother, and that I was supporting the Lancashire team on the day. We lost, but I'm over it now.

Castleford Tigers are playing at home this afternoon against a side from Perpignan, the Catalans Dragons, and my pub/hotel is clearly the favoured spot for Tigers fans to gather before and after the game to consider the finer points of the contest.

I leave my room at 3 o'clock and am in the ground by three minutes past (there was a queue.) Entry price is £22, which strikes me as pretty good compared with top flight footy – Castleford play in rugby league's top tier, known as Super League – and this comes down to £14 when I show my East Sussex bus pass. For an additional £3 I take a seat in the stands. There's free movement between the different parts of the ground which we don't see any more at football stadiums, so I can mingle with any Dragons fans if I want to practise my conversational Catalan. There are stands on three sides of the pitch and the open end has some basic looking hospitality boxes bearing the names of local firms.

The stadium itself now goes by the name of the Mend a Hose Jungle: the Jungle being the home of Tigers of course, while Mend a Hose, in the words of their website:

> …services, stocks and markets the widest range of fluid connector products available such as pneumatic and hydraulic fittings, quick couplings, rubber and thermoplastic hoses, and all associated requirements

…which, sadly, can't quite be accommodated on the rugby shirts of even the most heavily built forward.

Local rivals Wakefield (now, I believe, thankfully restored to "the Trinity" rather than the Trinity Wildcats) play at Rapid Solicitors Stadium. Featherstone Rovers are based at Bigfellas Stadium (the eponymous pizza firm also having naming rights to "Pontefract's Leading Nightclub" so they've got the social life of this part of West Yorkshire pretty well sorted) and Batley play hosts at Fox's Biscuits Stadium. But, in sponsorship terms, this season's big news has been the arrival on the rugby league scene of food giant Batchelors Peas. To quote the press launch:

Star players from each team went head-to-head at the Super League launch earlier this week in the 'Leaning Tower of Peas-a'challenge'… As well as building towers of cans, the players enjoyed a portion of fish, chips and mushy peas, and took a trip down memory lane to relive their childhood experiences of eating one of the country's best loved meals.

It was great to see the players getting involved and sampling Batchelors Peas – the perfect matchday must-have to accompany fish and chips. We're looking forward to involving players and fans in more mushy pea fun as the season progresses.

There's pre-match entertainment – no building towers of cans unfortunately, or legume-based hilarity – but the next best thing. It's the Junior, Intermediate and Senior Paws in turn – girls (I don't know if boys apply) performing cheerleader routines on the pitch with pompoms. The youngest look about four years old, the oldest perhaps thirteen or fourteen. According to the match day programme they train at the stadium every Wednesday and the training and performance bring fitness and self-esteem, which is surely right, and the subscriptions bring income to the club.

My seat is in the back row of the main stand, with a long line of press behind me armed with iPads and laptops. The ground can hold around 11,000 and today's attendance is announced as about half that, many of whom are wearing the Tigers' black and amber colours.

Just before kick-off, the Tiger and Dragon mascots emerge. They wouldn't frighten many, I feel. And it's time for the fifteen Castleford Tiger Claws to appear. These are the top, older dancers/cheerleaders (late teens I would think), dressed in black and all with very long hair. They form a pompom waving guard of honour as the teams come out.

And we're off!

An early try (not too technical yet, I hope?) to Castleford and the pompom girls do their thing on the touchline. An equalising score for the Dragons – no pompoms. Each score for the home side earns some pompom action; Dragons, not so.

Immediately behind me there's an excitable French reporter commentating to an audience somewhere near the Pyrenees and, from the decibel level, I wonder if he's forgotten to bring his technology with him and is relying on human voice alone. From my schoolboy French I think I recognise expressions equivalent to, "He's gone down very easy there" and, "This ref is a home banker", though I may have misheard that one.

It's good to see that rugby league fans are just as one-eyed as football supporters. I'm convinced that the chap in the seat to my right has a lucky shirt in Castleford's black and amber colours that he wore on a sweltering day earlier in the season when the Tigers started on a winning run and he's reluctant to change it in case it brings bad luck – it's just my bad luck that the winning run has continued for so long.

The Dragons have a player, Dave Taylor, who may not, I suspect, be Catalan himself but who is clearly auditioning for the part of "bad boy". He possesses an enormous backside which he deploys effectively for sitting or lying on opponents. This makes him unpopular with home fans, and unadmired by the referee.

The game finishes 38 to 24 to the Tigers so the fans are happy and depart to the strains of Neil Diamond's *Sweet Caroline* on a continuous loop. And my new friend on my right will be here wearing the same shirt next week.

Forecast: showers.

I chat with the landlord over breakfast. Paul has run the hotel for eight years. He tells me it's 150 years old. He moved from Yorkshire to Wales after the 1980s miners' strike because of the deep split in his community that it caused, but is now back on home territory. The Wheldale hotel is itself named after a local colliery, now closed of course. Paul shares my appreciation of *Brassed Off.*

I ask whether the planned relocation of the Tigers to a site on the edge of town will be bad for business, bearing in mind his pub seems to be a base for local support. He acknowledges there will be change and, as a Tigers fan himself, has mixed feelings. Fans who travel with visiting teams like coming to Castleford, he says, because it's a traditional ground, with far more character than the off-the-shelf new stadia. But fans are here for only a few hours before and after each game on fifteen days a year. On every match day, the staff clear everything in the bar to make room, which is why my friend Pete, checking in on the Saturday morning, had assumed that the builders were in and there would be no service. If the ground is redeveloped for housing, along with some of the empty sites around, that should mean a more regular clientele for the pub.

Paul can't attend home games as those are his busiest times, but he attends most away games. Not to Perpignan, I suggest, the home of yesterday's visiting team? But I'm wrong – it's a cheap and pleasant trip. While for Paul and the other fans of local, northern sides, an annual trip to faraway Perpignan is a one-off jolly each season, every away game in the north of England is something of a trek for the Catalan supporters – which explains the lack of visible Dragon fans at the game.

We agree that yesterday's result was a good one for the Tigers, leaving them well placed for the end of season play-offs. Paul feels that the narrow Castleford pitch counted against the Dragons and I'm in no position to comment.

I'm searching my map for the best route out of town, but Paul kindly offers to drop me somewhere convenient for my path.

I decide I need to be on the Aire and Calder canal rather than the River Aire as the latter looks very bendy on the map (bendy: that's a technical term used by us geographers) and I have a long way to go.

As soon as I get out of the car and unfold my map, a passer-by stops to ask if I'm lost, then points me towards the canal.

The cooling towers of Ferrybridge power station are behind me, those of Eggborough ahead. The midges are still biting. I'm mainly in open country on the canal bank but I'm within sight and sound of the M62 and there are pylons and numerous bridges over my path – rail, disused rail, major and minor roads, cable, pipeline.

I pass Kellingley colliery on my left. Opened only in 1965, it supplied coal to Ferrybridge and Drax power stations but closed towards the end of 2015, the last deep mine in the country, making 450 miners redundant. "End of an era" hardly does justice.

A heron keeps me company along the bank, staying just ahead of me. This is now a long, largely level walk across the Vale of York with long stints between bridges and nobody in sight. Large fields of wheat, drainage ditches, few hedges but the occasional wood. I eat the last of my liquorice and pork pies for lunch beneath a road bridge at Heck. If my wife were here she'd be wanting me to eat more veg, but she isn't, and you can't beat a bit of processed meat and gelatine on a canal path.

After lunch I carry on uninterrupted along the towpath for hours. This can test you mentally as well as physically.

Wheat fields. Vegetable fields of some sort. Cooling towers. Now there's something different, I'm leaving my map! Horror! I need to leave the canal to head to my overnight stop in Snaith, but I did have the sense last night to Google map the rest of the way and I think I can remember where I need to leave the towpath.

After three hours in a void without seeing a soul, I spot two women with dogs approaching on the far side of the canal, so

I shout across, "Excuse me! Can you tell me, am I nearing civilisation?" There follows a pause and a brief conversation between the women which I can't pick up, followed by, "Well, Snaith is just down the way."

I come off the towpath and walk north along the road, fortunately with pavement, past a pub (closed until evening, sadly), across the M62 then along a lane and a footpath into Snaith to avoid a long trudge on the main road. I pass a sign to Nancy's café which I can see in a shipping container in an industrial site 100 yards away. If it had been right on my road I'd have stopped, but 100 yards looks a long way and, at 3 p.m., it might be closed – my risk assessment concludes there is too great a possibility of disappointment and wasted effort, so I press slowly on.

Snaith looks different from the other Yorkshire towns I've been passing through this week. Largely brick built, not stone. Proper small shops. There are several pubs. I don't know how busy they'll be on a Monday night, or what they'll be serving, but unlike Castleford they're not boarded up. I'm booked into historic Downe Arms.

The name Snaith, I learn from information in my room, comes from a Scandinavian word meaning "piece of land cut off by rivers", though I can't see it myself. I don't think they had a word for "land squeezed between river and M62". It's been a busy medieval port and had a priory with its own ecclesiastical court. There were four church wardens at one time, one of whose duties was to enforce the wearing of woolly hats on Sundays or face a fine of fourpence.

It's sunny the next morning. I don't have a hat, woolly or otherwise, but it's only Tuesday.

I ordered breakfast last night as required but when I emerge from my room in the annex the main building is locked and in darkness. There's no response to bell or phone so I head off in search of sustenance. I get a café to make up a sandwich for later: it turns out to be enormous and objects to going in my sack.

It's lovely walking today. I decide to follow the river towards Goole rather than the canal. I see from my notes that my comments on the walking are always more positive in the mornings. Sky mainly blue but not too hot, a little breeze. Arable farming, fields of wheat. Poppies. Some very dark butterflies (Pete, where are you when I need you to identify stuff?). Award winning thistles and Himalayan balsam on the river bank. Solo wind turbines, cooling towers, a small windfarm, but everything fits into the landscape. People talk about "big skies" in places like this, and it looks great today. I don't get to talk much when I'm walking, other than to myself, so I stop to chat with two men working alongside an Environment Agency van and we agree that resources in the public sector are not what they were.

It's getting hot and I'm hatless. I do wish I had something. I douse one of my T-shirts with bottled water and tie it round my neck.

That might be the sound of a curlew. And there are swallows. The grass on the path is now three feet high and hard to walk through. The breeze has dropped and it's hotter. But I'm still glad I'm not wearing shorts – the long grass has a mean whipping action and there are hostile nettles camped round all the stiles.

I cut off a long river meander and risk the field footpaths. I meet a bull – I can see he has the relevant dangly bits. He's large and brown and horned, on his own and stood unreasonably close to the stile that I need to get to. On the other side of a small pond from him are around twenty cows and calves. I don't want to go back and follow the meander and I don't fancy barging straight up to him, so I walk slowly around the pond through his herd with one eye fixed on him and the other scanning the hedge for any weak points. There aren't any. I wonder how deep the pond is and I'm also asking myself if anybody knows I'm here. How many days before I'm missed. Seriously. The bull and I maintain mutual eye contact throughout, though I can't recall whether this is held to be a good thing and I don't want to stop and Google it. We're now an equal distance away from the stile, I'm banking on him not having worked out how to get over one of those, and I'm starting to offer myself shorter odds.

Reader, I'm here to tell the tale…

I reach Rawcliffe. It looks well-heeled and attractive, around a large village green with splendid trees and a church with a spire. I can see at least three pubs and they're all closed at lunchtime.

Fields of wheat and barley. Root crops. Some cattle (we've met, thank you). A few hedges, ditches, pylons, turbines solo and in small groups. There's a sign on the river bank, "Grass cutting in progress" which is not good news, not in the hay fever season.

I stop on the river bank to tackle my jumbo-sized butty and soon prove to be of great interest to clouds of flying insects. Goole is in sight now across the flat landscape. I continue along the river to Airmyn, another attractive settlement with a riverside esplanade. I turn into a housing estate then follow footpaths to join a wide arterial road into Goole with grassy verges and cycle and walking paths past a sign reading "Haven of Opportunity: The UK's Premier Inland Port".

I sit for a few minutes in West Park which has a nicely restored bandstand and pavilion – hoorah for the Heritage Lottery – then past well maintained terraced streets to a pedestrianised main shopping street with flower beds. I'll have time to explore Goole properly when I pick up from here next time but now I have a meeting arranged with the chair of the local civic society.

It's one thing joining an organisation committed to looking

after the best bits of somewhere like Beverley with its attractive shop fronts and teashops but, it seems to me, a tougher task if you're talking about Goole.

That's not something that discourages Margaret Hicks-Clarke. Margaret has lived in Goole since 2002, having moved here in connection with her work as a journalist with the Press Association in nearby Howden. From my own work, I'm very familiar with civic societies and the committed people who devote so much time and energy to their local community and the public realm.

In Margaret's case, when I press her, she tells me that – in addition to being chair of Goole Civic Society – she's a committee member of the Yorkshire and Humber Association of Civic Societies; sits on the executive board of Goole's Local Growth Partnership, which guides the strategy for the regeneration of the town; is a member of the Employment and Skills Board of the Humber Local Enterprise Partnership and a member of its Digital Sector Group. For good measure she is also a member of the York, North Yorkshire and East Riding Local Enterprise Partnership Skills and Employability Board.

In her spare time, she's a trustee of Castaway Accessible Music Theatre in Goole, which believes in the power of the arts to transform the lives of adults and young people with learning and physical disabilities, and she sings in the Goole-based Read's Warblers Show Choir. Oh, and she's also a governor of Selby College, just up the road.

Goole Civic Society, I learn, is five years old with just twenty members, most of whom Margaret describes as active on the organisation's behalf. Some are young with useful backgrounds in conservation, some are incomers who appreciate the attractions of the place and others are proud of the place they've lived all their lives. The initial momentum for setting up the organisation came from the owner of the Lowther Hotel (I'm booked to stay a night there on my next trip north), who objected to the demolition of an historic pub in Old Goole on the other side of the Dutch River after it was hit by a lorry. She felt that some kind of organisation was needed to alert the authorities and lobby effectively in the event of similar incidents.

The Society is active in commenting on planning applications and highlights the town's heritage and special qualities through publications, press releases, competitions and talks. Their first blue plaque in the town commemorated Percy Jeeves who played cricket for Goole, fifty first class games for Warwickshire between 1912 and 1914, and for the Players against the Gentlemen at the Oval. P.G. Wodehouse said that he named his famous valet after Percy having seen him playing at Cheltenham in 1913. Jeeves died in action at the Somme in 1916 aged 28.

Membership of the Society may be small, and it has no paid staff (the equivalent civic society in my own town, with a population slightly smaller than Goole, has ten times the number of members) but it continues to secure funds for projects from various sources and plans to get involved with Hull's year as UK City of Culture. Margaret is upbeat about the Society going forward. But then, I'm beginning to feel it might be hard to find Margaret when she's not in an upbeat mood.

My train homewards is approaching and it's time to leave. I'll be back soon.

Chapter 8

Heatstroke on the Humber

A fortnight ago I wrenched my left knee accomplishing the tricky task of getting out of bed. Whether it would have been audible had anyone been within earshot, I know not, but it seemed loud from where I was. This was worrying as the knee is not my own. Rather, I suppose it is now, but it came as a gift about nine years ago from you, via the wonderful NHS. (I'm worth it; I use the knee quite a bit and take it everywhere.) The medicine man in my town thought the wrenching sound might not involve a failure in the replacement parts but in my remaining inherited infrastructure, and that rest might do it good.

So, here I am on the train approaching Goole with a sore and swollen knee, just so you don't think this has all been fun. I can't help but notice that the turbines appear to have bred since I was here a month ago.

From Goole station, I set off walking to the docks and the Yorkshire Waterways Museum, whose mission is to, "use the heritage, arts and environment of the Yorkshire waterways as a resource for learning and regeneration". I'm meeting the director of the Sobriety Project, which is based here.

Paul Cooper and I sit outside the museum with a mug of tea and a view of the Aire and Calder Navigation. Paul explains that *Sobriety* is the name of the blue and white painted canal boat moored nearby. From the website, I'd worked out that the project wasn't about alcohol but not where the name came from. I'm given a helpful potted history of canal restoration since the low point of the 1950s and how a local businessman in the early 1970s, remembering his own enjoyment of canals when young, bought *Sobriety* to take young people on boat trips to stimulate an interest in the outdoors and instil life skills.

By 1980, *Sobriety* was operating as a charity, additional boats were acquired, day and overnight trips were organised, and staff employed. The 1990s saw the building that we're sitting outside begin its life as a base for the charity, funded largely from other charities. Associated British Ports (ABP), who run the port of Goole, provide help in kind, enabling Sobriety to develop its activity programmes. Paul joined around that time; with a background in care homes and with a knowledge of boats, he started as a skipper and is now the charity's director.

The project's collection of artefacts grew into a museum devoted to the local waterways, providing an additional resource for visiting groups. With funding available through the lottery, European Social Fund and European Regional Development Fund, Sobriety acquired more boats and developed an outreach programme in Selby and Thorne. Other charities furnished many of the clients and in 2001, with Heritage Lottery funding, the museum opened in the form that I can see today.

Sobriety uses its museum, waterways and boats, community gardens and allotments, nature trail, engineering and woodwork shops, and the healthy eating café as resources for personal development for disadvantaged people. These include: young people excluded or at risk of exclusion from school; men and their families resettling from a custodial sentence; adults with learning and physical disabilities; people with mental health issues; and those suffering from the effects of unemployment, low income or rural isolation. The project provides training programmes, work experience and volunteering opportunities.

There is currently a core of a dozen full and part-time staff based at the museum and more than a hundred volunteers. Most volunteers are local people, not all of them interested in boats but enjoying the company and wanting to contribute. They are of three types – the "traditional" retired members of the community, some in poor health, with time to spare and skills to offer; those who have previously participated in Sobriety schemes as clients and may themselves have learning difficulties; inmates from a men's open prison near Thorne on day release, often skilled and diligent and seeking a reintroduction to work.

Economic recession has hit the project – through cuts in local authority budgets, a reduction in what the public is prepared to contribute, and in the funding available to other charities to bring their clients here. Boat occupancy has fallen. Sobriety is seeking business sponsorship and expertise; public boat trips are run around the docks. As with all of the projects that I've visited on this walk, the future is always uncertain. The Big Lottery and the Heritage Lottery Fund are currently supporting vital programmes, but these are time limited. Sobriety is obliged to keep its eyes and ears out for the latest announcements of politicians in order to shape its next round of funding bids: will there be resources for mental health, or for offenders' programmes?

It's now late afternoon and the museum is closing. I take the opportunity for a quick tour of the excellent exhibits and displays before Paul drives me to my hotel on his way home. I'm booked into the most historic hotel (indeed, the most historic anything) in town. Elsewhere on this walk I've favoured old station hotels where they exist: here I've gone for the dockland equivalent.

The hotel was built in 1824 and was the very first building in Goole, two years before the port was opened. This is not a pretty harbour but a major inland port, 45 miles from the North Sea at the junction of the rivers Don and Ouse, upstream from the point where the Ouse meets the River Trent to form the Humber estuary. Originally built for the export of coal from the Yorkshire coalfields, this was where cargo was transhipped onto seagoing vessels. Amongst the imports travelling in the opposite direction were timber pit props for the mines. Loose cargo has been replaced by container traffic, mainly with Europe, and the port remains a thriving concern with three miles of quayside and eight functioning docks lined with transit sheds and adorned with huge overhead cranes and the iconic "salt and pepper pot" water towers. "Salt" is brick built from 1885, "pepper" is concrete from 1927: both are Grade II listed and distinctive landmarks in the town. Since the closure of the Yorkshire coalmines and their demand for pit props, the former Timber Pond near the Waterways Museum is now a marina with berths for 150 boats.

To accompany the development of the port, a new town was laid out on a gridiron pattern and Goole's population (just 450 in 1826 when the port opened), grew rapidly and now stands at 18,000. An informal twinning arrangement between the town and Gibraltar, initiated in the 1960s, appears to have faded, no doubt when Spain's aggressive territorial ambitions for Goole receded.

My hotel, the Lowther, was bought by the Aire and Calder Navigation Company (the people who built the port) in 1828 and later named after their first chairman. They used rooms on the first floor as their boardroom and chairman's office where they had murals painted. These have recently been rediscovered and restored and I pop in for a viewing. The murals are views of Goole and its brand-new docks in 1828 from the other side of the river and are delightful works both of art and industrial archaeology.

After dinner at the Lowther (it's a quiet night in Goole, just me in the restaurant), I go for a wander. The old market hall looks impressive from the outside, the pedestrianised shopping street appears to have an abundance of nail salons, charity and pawn shops, and there are a number of bars around the town centre, mainly quiet on this Thursday evening. I call in at the Drake and order a pint of Rudgate's Ruby Mild, which proves very user friendly, and I'm impressed to see bitter at £1.98 a pint, which would be the subject of ancient myth and folklore back in Sussex.

I pass the time over my pint by reading a leaflet produced by the local Civic Society that I picked up at the museum; a short guide to the town. This includes the nugget that, if you Google Goole, the search engine asks, "Did you mean 'google'?", which is a bit cheeky. I do Google Goole and learn that, without actually moving, the town has been in three different counties since 1974 (West Riding of Yorkshire, Humberside and East Riding), which is cool.

I head back to the hotel along Aire Street. While it leads to the docks and must once have been at the heart of the town, the road now feels somewhat out on a limb and has seen better days. Hotels have closed, and premises have been boarded up, with just the odd takeaway doing business. The Lowther is at the far end of the street. Opposite, on the dock wall, is a copy of a painting of a coal sloop on the Humber, *Masterman*, by Reuben Chappell, the Pierhead Painter. This is the beginning of an art trail around the town devised by the Civic Society to celebrate the work of Chappell who was born a stone's throw from the docks in 1870 and spent his lifetime painting portraits of vessels, often commissioned by their owners or shipbuilders. He had plenty of practice. It's estimated that he painted up to 12,000 of them.

Before I head to my room I spot a sign in Reception alerting guests that there will be loud music in the Voodoo Chilli cocktail bar on Fridays and Saturdays until 3 a.m. I'm pleased this is Thursday as I'm not sure I'm a Voodoo Chilli kind of chap. Unless it's a crisp flavour that I've not come across.

I restrict myself to a modest breakfast as I'm (slowly) learning the lesson that a stomach overloaded with carbs and saturated fats and subsequent exercise don't mix. I have what I know will be the longest walk of my whole trek today – something like 14 miles if all goes to plan. There doesn't appear to be any accommodation along my route from Goole to Hull so I'm booked into a spa hotel a couple of miles off the path. The weather's fine but my knee hurts.

A closer look at my Ordnance Survey map tells me that my intended route out of town would require me to be a train, as the bridge over the river in the direction of Hull has no provision for anyone except trains. This is not a good start. I don't fancy the additional four mile walk to reach the far side of the river on foot via Boothferry Bridge, so I phone for a taxi to take me as far as the bridge where I can pick up the river bank path, adding just two miles to my intended route. This is two miles that I may later come to regret.

Boothferry Bridge was the lowest crossing point of the river, that is the nearest to the North Sea, before the construction of the Humber Bridge close to Hull in 1981, and I'm hazarding a guess that there may have been a ferry at Boothferry before there was a bridge. Hull, on the north side of the wide Humber estuary, close to the coast and with no fixed crossing of the estuary before 1981, must have felt closer to ports overseas than it did to much of the UK.

My taxi driver is from Latvia and doesn't seem keen to chat about the EU referendum. He drops me close to the bridge at the

Ferry Boat Inn and I set off along the raised north bank of the River Ouse, past large flat fields with a fine crop of turbines and beneath the M62. The walking is good but it's already uncomfortably warm and I'm hatless. Sunshine shimmers on the river and there are small wading birds on the mud. Half a dozen geese graze on the bank amongst a flock of sheep and a tiny vole dashes across my path.

I pass a sewage works and a depot of shiny green lorries and low loaders belonging to a kitchen and bedroom business and walk through a small industrial estate to Howdendyke, a hamlet of well maintained, redbrick terraced houses labelled Ferry Row and Tutty Row. I can guess why Ferry Row but Tutty and I aren't on first name terms. The dictionary gives me "an impure oxide of zinc obtained from the flues of smelting furnaces", which makes a nice change from Hollyhock Cottage, I suppose. My route takes me back to the river bank and a minor road southward past expensive looking houses with fine views of Himalayan balsam, an attractive little parish church and several farms to the eastern end of the railway bridge over the Ouse which I'd intended to walk across from Goole first thing this morning before I paid proper attention to the map. That's one and a half hours and, according to my pedometer, over 8,500 steps already in hot sun and I'm now at the planned start point for the longest day's walk of my entire trek. Bugger.

At least I'm now heading eastwards towards the coast, past Saltmarshe Delph, a nature reserve managed by Yorkshire Wildlife Trust. A pair of swans with two gorgeous, almost full sized, downy cygnets approach to be fed. I move on past a van labelled Equine Agronomist. The driver parks and takes his dogs for a walk. He's dressed like a scoutmaster with the sort of shorts that, if he were married, his wife would ban.

In contrast to the early stages of my walk in Liverpool and

Manchester in late spring, this is becoming uncomfortably hot and I'm flagging. I walk on through Saltmarshe Park, formal parkland dotted with mature trees including some spectacular copper beeches, the road lined with horse chestnuts. A sign tells me that some of the land alongside my route at Dairy Farm (sounds like The Archers) is in "Higher Level Stewardship", in receipt of government funding in return for conservation friendly management and public access. Saltmarshe Hall itself is attracting a fair number of visitors today as its gardens have been opened to the public. But it's not right on my route, so: no.

I have a rest and a banana on a broad grassy bank overlooking a sweep of the river by some expensive looking houses. There's a man from the Environment Agency operating a radio-controlled mower on the slopes of the river bank. I notice, as he deftly steers it back across the road and onto his trailer, that it's shredding the tarmac with its blades and I wonder if he's aware. Perhaps that's not his problem.

The Trans Pennine Trail that I'm following now leaves the minor road for the first time since Howdendyke to continue eastwards on top of the river bank. There's an attractive line of houses along the far bank. The walking now is, well, perfect. A level gradient, an even surface of smooth, soft grass – hoorah for the Environment Agency and its dodgy mowers looking after the path for us walkers and cyclists – and a helpful breeze.

Ah, it couldn't last. Half a mile along, I reach the first intake from the river, beyond which the mowing regime abruptly ends, and I'm faced with grass three feet deep. The mowing is clearly for the purposes of maintaining the bank only; sod the walkers and the cyclists. I'm ploughing my own way through the vegetation and I'm glad I put in my eye drops this morning.

I'm presented with a dilemma. There's one of those temporary notices pinned to a post by East Riding Council telling me of a closure of the footpath a mile or more ahead so that maintenance works can be carried out. But there's no date given for completion. The diversion will involve a miserable detour and extra mileage which I can ill afford. But if I press on and the path is still closed I'll have to retrace my steps and that'll be far worse. Sod it. Nobody told me that my trek would raise such existential questions. With the kind of spirit that guided those explorers of yesteryear – Scott, Shackleton, Hillary, Ant and Dec – I press on. And I'm in luck. The works have finished. Or not started. The way is open to the orient.

The Wolds appear in the distance to the north. Cereal crops are awaiting harvest or have just been brought in. Fields have been ploughed for a winter crop of turbines. There's an actual lighthouse on the far bank of the river. I didn't know that rivers had those.

I'm confronted by hundreds of sheep approaching along the bank. They're white with mottled faces but amongst them there are two groups – each of four black sheep with white faces and feet – keeping together, surrounded by the white ones. I feel there may be something significant about this, but I don't know what it is. Anyway, it's very hot.

In this quiet location it's a surprise to see that someone has erected an information board about "warp land" (where turbid river water is allowed to flood the farmland in order to improve it), about the origin of place names like fen (waterlogged terrain), ing (waterlogged terrain), carr (waterlogged terrain with some trees) and dyke (ditch, to reduce the amount of waterlogged terrain). And about Cornelius Vermuyden, a Dutch engineer (or benefit scrounging asylum seeker as we would now describe him while showing him the door) who supervised the draining of all those ings, carrs and fens.

The Hope and Anchor is open! I order a pint of lime and

lemon, a packet of salted nuts and a bottle of water to go: a balanced lunch in anyone's book.

There's still a light breeze but I am definitely feeling the effects of sunstroke. I'm tiring, I'm slowing noticeably and there's no shade at all on the river bank. Humberside in August. It's like the Med in a heatwave. The Ouse Valley Riviera.

A planning application notice on a fence at Faxfleet announces an intention to create avocet habitat on Whitton Island where the rivers Ouse and Trent meet to form the Humber. Dealing with the application must be a bit more interesting for the planning case officer than the run of the mill house extensions. What conditions do you attach to the avocet permission in terms of building materials?

There's barley in the fields. Or it could be wheat. Pete's not here to tell me and, in truth, I'm past caring. For the past couple of hours, I've been thinking of little other than my dwindling water supply and the complete absence of shade and I'm moving more and more slowly. If there were any hope of a lift, I'd take it.

When I discovered that there was no accommodation on my route between Goole and Hull, it left the option of an (for me) unmanageable walk of 30 miles, or diverting a couple of miles north from my path to a spa hotel. I reasoned it might cost no more to spend a night there than phoning for a taxi to take me back to Goole or onwards to Hull, and back again in the morning. My plan was to arrive mid-afternoon and make use of facilities like the hotel pool as a reward for a long day. In reality, I'm struggling into the landscaped grounds of the hotel, making no more than one mile an hour, at about six o'clock – too tired, too stiff and suffering from the heat too much to make use of anything. My pedometer registers 40,000 steps for the day.

I cut an awkward figure leaning sickly and sweatily with my own cloud of midges on the hotel's reception desk while all around me a wedding reception is in full flow. I make it to my room and fall onto the bed, not to shift for several hours. I send down for a sandwich and don't even finish the crisps. From my bed, I watch the Olympic Games from Rio on the TV. As I slide into deep slumber, I hear myself being interviewed by Clare Balding in the press zone and I'm telling her about the sacrifices I've made to be here tonight. And how it hasn't been worth it.

I'm never going to move again.

They don't sell hats in my hotel and there are no shops nearby. There's a shower cap in my bathroom. I try it on and send my wife a picture, but I don't think it will help much if it's as hot today as it was yesterday. I check my phone for email and social media and catch up with all the news from "Friends" that I didn't know I'd got. I'm heading down for breakfast when I catch sight of myself in a mirror and realise that I'm still wearing the shower cap which seems inappropriate.

I take a taxi back to my riverside path. It's breezy this morning, for which, many thanks. And it's coming from behind me so that's a bonus. There are information panels about European wildlife designations and the Roman settlement of Brough and there is a splendid view across the Humber estuary, its marsh and mudflats. It's deeply impressive; not pretty but handsome. Grey in the morning light, a broad, grey river and a big, grey sky. A grand sweep of farmland with its turbine-scape, pylons and riverside industry. When I hear people talk about big skies I assume they mean the landscape is, well, flat and boring but this morning I understand. My gaze returns time and again to this view through the rest of my walk to the coast. My kind of river, the Humber. There should be songs about it.

I pass the BAE, or British Aerospace, factory alongside the river, then a large sailing lake with a solitary water skier. The Humber Bridge is in sight ahead of me but that doesn't mean I've nearly reached it. I'll aim to be there by lunchtime.

A nudge from behind and a wet nose on the back of my hand turns out to mean I'm being overtaken by a dog walker, which is a relief. We wander along together while he enthuses about the local countryside as a backdrop for his walks. It's the first company I've had for a while but after two fields he turns off towards his car and I choose a low-level route across the pebbly, muddy shore over a high tide route along the bank.

At North Ferriby there is a pleasantly landscaped area, information about bronze age boats discovered there and seats provided by Reckitt and Coleman. The name registers as I'm aware that the firm is still a major business locally and has long established links with the community. I plan to see Sir James Reckitt's garden village when I reach Hull. From here I'm following the parish council's riverside walkway to the Humber Bridge and the views across the Humber are superb.

It's hot again today (nobody warned me about Humberside in the summer) and I'm grateful for a drink at the Country Park Hotel beneath the bridge. I'm in Hessle and the area has something of a resort feel on a sunny Saturday, with a grassy promenade and an ice cream van and the Yorkshire Wolds Way and the Trans Pennine Trail passing through. There are pleasant cottages old and new, and have I mentioned the views?

The resort bit doesn't extend far and I'm soon picking my way through an office park and thick undergrowth alongside the main road from the Humber Bridge to Hull city centre – Clive Sullivan Way – named after a local legend of rugby league. If the term "legend" is casually used these days – denoting someone who spends two weeks in the Big Brother house or the local butcher who stocks your favourite sausages – it's no exaggeration in Sullivan's case. Following an army career, Sullivan achieved the kinds of record in the game that won't be equalled. He was the first black captain of any British national sporting side, some six years before the first black player was picked for England's senior (association) football team. Under his captaincy the British Rugby League team won the 1972 World Cup – a feat they haven't managed to repeat. He played 352 games for Hull FC between 1961 and 1973 and, amazingly in a city divided firmly down the middle between its two great sides, another 213 times for arch rivals Hull Kingston Rovers between 1974 and 1981. Clive died from cancer aged 42 – in Hull. A dual carriageway is the least he deserved.

I'm arriving in Hull for the first time in my life (which feels something of a landmark), following the edge of the Humber along St. Andrew's Quay. First there's waste land where, I presume, something has been demolished or filled in, then an extensive modern retail park complete with McDonald's, Subway and the rest. My mobile rings and, as that hasn't happened since Dewsbury, I can't recall where it is. It turns out to be Mac who supported me earlier on the walk and has phoned to congratulate me as he thinks this is the very last day of my coast to coast journey. When I outline my struggle of the previous day, he expresses surprise that I didn't think of calling a taxi. I remember now, that when we did our long coastal walks together years ago, it was the cream teas and the pints in the evening that held Mac's attention rather than the walk itself. But his is a helpful call as this is the time of day when the legs, and everything else, tend to give way and it's good to find, when the call finishes, that I'm that bit nearer my hotel.

Immediately beyond the retail park is a scarily derelict part of the old quay and I'm walking between the river and abandoned warehouses that would be perfect for the fingernail pulling scene in a particularly vicious crime thriller. As I tread warily round manholes that would precipitate me into the mudflats beneath, I'm conscious that absolutely nobody knows I'm here.

I hear voices and hope they're (a) human and (b) on my side. I turn a corner, aware that I'm in no state to run, and come face to face with two young couples with a buggy and a friendly dog on a lead. They're admiring *that* view over the river from a well-tended memorial bedecked with fresh flowers. It's a memorial to local trawlermen lost to the sea when fishing the waters around Greenland, Iceland and Murmansk, as well as those killed by enemy action in wartime. Despite the incongruous setting and difficult, rubbish and rubble-strewn approach, this is clearly a place of local pilgrimage and respect.

From here my route runs between the Albert Dock and the river. I'm separated from the dock by a high chain link fence and from the Humber by very little. After the dereliction this is more reassuring but just as quiet. Plenty of cargo vessels and clearly a functioning dock, but not a soul in sight. (May I also say, this being a fishing port, not a sole in sight? Thought not.) It feels just as eerie as the abandoned part of the quay, but I meet one young man approaching from the other direction. He's wearing a Brazil football shirt and reassures me that there is an exit from the walkway into the city centre across the dock entrance without my making a three-mile retreat. This is the kind of thing that looms large in my thoughts at the moment.

He's right. I leave the dock via a footbridge and boardwalk above warehouse roofs. I've arrived at the edge of the city centre and it's a short walk to my hotel past the Ice Arena in a very tired looking grey metal construction (or is it plastic sheeting?), an indoor bowls venue in a fine old redbrick building and the Whittington and Cat, with its gorgeous Victorian tiles, wood and etched glass.

I'm staying at the Royal Station Hotel, located unsurprisingly next to the Paragon railway station. Both station and hotel date from 1847 and are in splendid Italian Renaissance style with Doric and Ionic columns. I squeeze through to reception past the bridesmaids and ushers of a Saturday afternoon wedding party clustered at the entrance, all catching up urgently on missed cigarette time before the dinner and speeches.

I'm not up to sightseeing this evening and I'll have tomorrow to begin my exploration of the city. So, it's around the corner for a Saturday night curry. I see there's a large Mecca Bingo almost opposite the hotel. Now, that would be a first. I poke my head into the lobby and ask if there's any instruction leaflet I can pick up, for future interest. How hard can it be?

A plaque by the lift in the hotel tells me that Queen Victoria slept here. And typically jolly words from the Philip Larkin poem *Friday Night at the Royal Station Hotel* are inscribed on a plaque by the entrance:

> Light spreads darkly downwards from the high
> Clusters of lights over empty chairs
> That face each other, coloured differently.
> Through open doors, the dining-room declares
> A larger loneliness of knives and glass
> And silence laid like carpet. A porter reads
> An unsold evening paper. Hours pass,
> And all the salesmen have gone back to Leeds,
> Leaving full ashtrays in the Conference Room.

The ashtrays are no more, which is why the smoking bridesmaids are reduced to hanging around on the steps outside. In the station immediately behind the hotel there's a statue to Larkin who was employed as librarian at Hull University from 1955 until his death thirty years later. There's also a Larkin Trail linking places in the city associated with him.

I'm off this morning to see a little of what is, for me, a whole new city. Paragon Square in front of the hotel isn't the best of introductions. The branches of House of Fraser and TJ Hughes hail from a hasty post-war reconstruction after massive bomb damage (only 5,945 of the city's 92,660 houses were undamaged) but might have benefitted from a more measured approach. The centre is clearly being titivated for Hull City of Culture and the main shopping streets are awash with roadworks bearing the words "Destination Hull: 2017 and Beyond: Building a Legacy: You can forget about getting to the shops" (actually the last bit's mine).

Much has been made of Hull's status as the "winner" in the book *Crap Towns: The 50 Worst Places to Live in the UK*, pushing Cumbernauld into second place. Nominated in the book (and that by its own residents), for its high rates of unemployment, crime and heroin addiction, the smell of fish from Grimsby docks, the aroma of rotting carcasses and rancid flesh from the tanning factory and "*the silent threat of violence*", the city's entry concludes "*no matter what happens to me in later life, I will know that it can never, never be as bad as living in Hull.*"

But another contributor claims in those pages that Hull, along with Liverpool, is one of the friendliest places he's lived in, where "*People talk to each other, yes really, strangers and everything.*"

Which means, if I'm OK with the smell of fish and, er, the other stuff, I'm in for a good time.

The city is making a huge effort to rebrand itself as a business location and tourist destination and City of Culture is playing a big part. Hull is rediscovering what it has that's special and is keen to tell the world. There's plenty to tell. Information boards are springing up, highlighting the city's colourful history and maritime connections.

I'm heading for the old town that largely escaped the wartime blitz, with its cobbled streets, characterful old pubs, warehouses and staithes (wharves) along the River Hull just above its confluence with the Humber. But first I make my way through the shopping area. There's a modern mall built above the waters of Princes Quay and a scattering of fine buildings around the modern city. There's 19th and early 20th century grandeur around Queen Victoria Square in the form of City Hall, the Maritime Museum, Ferens Art Gallery and the Gothic and Jacobean extravaganza that is Punch Hotel. The helpful Tourist Information Centre is open even though it's Sunday.

Then there's the Land of Green Ginger. You could love a place merely on the strength of having a city centre street with a name like that. I decide to make the deli at the end of this short street my lunch stop. I study the long list of sandwich options on the blackboard while the owner chats with another customer about the holiday she's just back from.

"What would you like?" she asks me pleasantly.

"I'll have a prawn mayo with salad on brown, and tea please."

"Take a seat and I'll bring it through." She disappears into the kitchen and I settle down with my newspaper.

"I'm afraid I don't have any prawns. Sorry about that. Anything else I can get you?"

I go back to the counter and take another look at the blackboard.

"The pulled pork please. On brown."

Two minutes later. "We don't have any pulled pork either. Sorry."

I return to the blackboard. "Ham salad? On brown please."

Another two minutes pass. "I'm afraid the brown bread is a bit hard. I'm just back from holiday and it's in the freezer. Sorry."

"White will be fine, thanks." I omit to ask where the white bread has come from.

When I pass by later in the afternoon on my way back to the hotel, I notice a sign in the window replacing the one that said "Open". It now reads "I'm away on holiday. Back soon."

From here it's a short walk into the old town and its "museum quarter", with the Streetlife Museum, Hull and East Riding Museum, the Arctic Corsair berthed in the River Hull, and the William Wilberforce house all within a few yards of each other.

Museums have obviously come a long way in recent times and both the Streetlife (with an emphasis on transport and the traditional street scene) and the Hull and East Riding Museum (local history, natural history and archaeology) are quite brilliant in their displays and user friendliness. I'm not too bothered about taking in heavyweight information, though there's plenty to read, so much as being engaged by simple stories and having my appetite whetted. There's a display on the laying waste of settlements, the land and local livelihoods known as the "Harrying of the North" under William the Conqueror which, it seems, was never rivalled until the 1980s under Margaret Thatcher.

Perhaps because I've been involved with environmental information and interpretation and in hunting down the necessary funds, I notice the small boards that tell me just how much here was funded through the EU. In the Hull and East Riding Museum many of the galleries on local happenings have a comparator showing what was taking place elsewhere in the world at the same time, which can have a humbling effect. There are also constant reminders of Hull as a gateway to influences to and from abroad which makes the local "Leave EU" vote a sad one.

The name William Wilberforce has hovered over this walk since the Anti-Slavery gallery in Liverpool's Albert Dock. Exploring the houses of people you know something about has always been more interesting to me than merely gazing at the baubles and trappings of wealth in some anonymous stately home, and WW was surely a "good thing", as Sellar and Yeatman might have said. Touring his family home here in Hull, I learn that Wilberforce opposed the creation of trade unions, with which a later Hullensian, John Prescott MP, might have taken issue, and he supported various legislation that restricted people's rights, but we'll try to overlook that in the light of his better-known achievements. I also discover that, "There was always a great Yorkshire pie in his rooms," according to a friend, the Rev Thomas Gisborne. Which suggests he had a sense of priorities.

Not content merely to laud Wilberforce's key role in the abolition of the Atlantic slave trade, there's a good deal of material in the house about modern slavery and human rights, about discrimination, the African diaspora, and racism in football. There's a Wilberforce Institute for the Study of Slavery and Emancipation at the University of Hull and an annual Wilberforce Lecture which celebrates the historic role of the city "in combating the abuse of Human Rights personified in the work of the abolitionist William Wilberforce". Hull has been twinned since 1980 with Freetown, the capital of Sierra Leone.

The Nelson Mandela Gardens provide a foreground to the museums. There's a bronze bust of Mahatma Gandhi and, on a plaque, an extract from a speech made in Hull by Sir Shridath "Sonny" Ramphal, Commonwealth Secretary General in 1983. It reads:

I invite each and every one of you, citizens of Hull and other friends, to question whether any can take pride in the work and achievements of Wilberforce and the Anti-Slavery Movement if as individuals, as a nation, as a world community, we fail to take a righteous and uncompromising stand against apartheid. By what quirk of logic, what twist of values, can we celebrate emancipation and tolerate apartheid? We tarnish and depreciate the memory of Wilberforce so long as slavery South Africa style flaunts its evil and defies our will to curb it, sensing our resolve to be a fragile thing.

The UK government was alone at that time amongst the Commonwealth nations in declining to adopt economic sanctions against the South African regime.

From the museum quarter it's a short stroll up Scale Lane Staith, a landscaped street with art on a maritime theme, to Scale Lane Bridge, the newest crossing of the River Hull. It's for pedestrians and reconnects the city centre and old town with a rundown area and dockland on the east side of the river. There's a new hotel on the far side, currently somewhat surrounded by wasteland, and there's The Deep, but that's for tomorrow. The footbridge itself is fun (I'm easily excited). It pivots at the western end and you can stay on it when it swings open! From the bridge there's one of those industrial views that I get a kick out of: a series of bridges over the River Hull receding into the distance and a line of old warehouses on the west bank, once the economic heart of the city and now, as the "old town", one of the drivers for regeneration.

I walk back to the hotel through Queen Victoria Square and the shopping area, but the sound of live music draws me down an alley into a courtyard where there's a small stage, a sound system, a band playing Irish music and a beer tent, which is what a city needs on a Sunday afternoon. There's also a tent housing a contemporary art display and an exhibit that's part of a festival devoted to the memory of one of the city's most celebrated citizens, aviator Amy

Johnson. This is the 75th anniversary of Amy's death and Hull isn't going to let that pass without a bit of a do.

Evening is quiet in the city centre. As in Wakefield and Castleford, people seem to entertain themselves at home these days rather than filling the pubs, and dining out appears to have relocated to the retail parks.

By taxi to Hull's garden suburb, or village, just off Holderness Road. The driver is English and, though he works here, he has moved house to Beverley. As he overtakes one of the little road trains which tour the city centre, I ask him about Hull.

"It's on the road to nowhere," he tells me.

"You think it's a good thing, City of Culture, bringing people to the place?"

"Nah."

"But, you know, attracting tourists, good for business...?"

"If anyone comes, they'll be disappointed."

"But, when they've been to something in the programme, they may want to come back another time, explore the area?"

"Not once they've been, they won't."

"Oh look, we've arrived."

I've spoken to a few taxi drivers on this side of the Pennines during my trips north and they all seemed quite upbeat and chatty. I think this has been the first obvious Englishman.

Sir James Reckitt, owner of the big starch and chemical company of that name, was a Quaker and, in creating Hull's garden village (1907 to 1913) inspired by the Garden City movement, he was following in the footsteps of fellow Quaker industrialists, George Cadbury and Joseph Rowntree. Reckitt announced his plan to "establish a Garden Village, within a reasonable distance of our Works, so that those who are wishful might have the opportunity of living in a better house, with a garden, for the same rent that they now pay for a house in Hull – with the advantages of fresher air, and such Clubs, and outdoor amusements, as are usually found in rural surroundings." It's not clear what clubs or rural amusements he had in mind but I'm sure they were just fine.

There are twelve tree-lined streets or avenues of brick built, often pebble dashed, houses with steeply pitched roofs and overhanging eaves, a mix of curves and straight lines; most are named after trees or shrubs. The original village included a shopping centre, club house, a hostel for female workers and several almshouses. The Garden Village Company was disbanded in 1950 and now most of the facility buildings have gone or been converted to dwellings, the village is embedded in the urban spread of the city and most passers-by may be unaware of the existence of this pioneering venture. But a substantial number of the remaining buildings are now protected by being "listed" and the village became Hull's first conservation area in 1970.

From here, on to The Deep, which is just an aquarium in the same way that the Shard in London is just an office block. It's on the east side of the River Hull at the point where it flows into the Humber, and it's big. It must be one of the top visitor attractions, not just in Hull, but for miles around, with: vast tanks containing fish and other sea creatures; penguins; sharks; and some very strange things you wouldn't want to meet even in your dreams. It's clearly not just a tourist attraction: there are serious eco-messages being narrated here, and The Deep is an active partner in research on the conservation of marine habitats like corals. According to the entertaining and informative labels, Amphioxus "prefers to spend its time buried in the sand in tropical lagoons", with which one can empathise, while "If attacked, the Sea Cucumber can shoot out its stomach and leave it behind". And who wouldn't wish for that as their superpower?

A walk back now to the station for my train home. I try Cooplands Quality Bakers for a sandwich on the way. There's a full list of possibilities on the board and I go for a chicken and bacon roll, which is hot and is prepared in front of me, with fresh salad and garlic mayo. They tell me I can have it as part of a "meal deal" with a tea and choice of pie (I like the look of the sausage roll) and that comes to £3. This is my kind of sandwich shop. I take my lunch into Queens Gardens, once a dock reaching right into the heart of the city and now an attractive stretch of grass and flower beds, full of Hullensians enjoying the summer sun. The city is looking good. And my £3 was money well spent.

Chapter 9

Once More Unto the Breach: Bingo,
Genevieve and a Lost Town

It's September and I'm back in Hull to start the sixth and final stage of my walk to the coast. I've already seen something of the city, but I have a few more things on my list. This afternoon I'm at the Beverley Road Baths.

For someone who's not much of a swimmer I have an unreasonable enthusiasm for Victorian, Edwardian and 1930s baths and, along with certain railway termini, believe they represent some of the best of British architecture. Hull can take credit for being Britain's first local authority after Liverpool (there's that link again) to provide public baths with swimming facilities. The city has two surviving examples of baths from the turn of the 19th century. I can tell from the photos and written descriptions that the East Hull Baths on Holderness Road have a superb frontage with alternate brick and yellow terracotta bands and a wrought iron balcony, but I've opted for Beverley Road and I'm not disappointed.

Assistant Manager Sue Joyce gives me a conducted tour. Sue is a local and has worked at Beverley Road for five years. She's clearly proud of the place, which feels warm and inviting, and that's not something I associate automatically with old swimming baths. It underwent a restoration 25 years ago with many of the original features retained – Baroque frontage, sumptuous main entrance hall, visible iron trusses, tiles, art nouveau doorways, stained glass, mosaics, gallery seating, balcony railings. The main pool has been divided, with a small training pool at one end and 25 metres left for "proper swimming". The old second pool now accommodates the filtration equipment and won't be put back to water.

Beverley Road recently accommodated a 60th wedding anniversary celebration for a couple who met there at a dance in the days when pools were routinely covered over for football, concerts or ballroom – the baths still serving at the heart of the community.

I'm heading this evening to Mecca Bingo, opposite the Royal Station Hotel where I'm staying again. The last time I played bingo was probably a Sunday afternoon in front of the fire after dinner and I had a card with blue and white squares and a stack of little cardboard pieces to cover the numbers. It was about 1955 and I expect things may have changed.

Mecca occupy a 1950s building, the former Cecil Theatre. I don't want to embarrass myself with my ignorance, so I've done some research via Mecca's website. I'm encouraged by the exhortation "Bingo is like theatre; it has a beginning, a middle and an end."

There's clearly a significant online bingo community. Kirsty has been voted Chat Moderator of the Month, something which probably deserves wider recognition. And those employed at the "hard copy" (built) venues are not forgotten. There are votes for favourite callers and helpful staff and I learn that "Lucie deserves to go higher in the bingo world".

The website has a page on "Lost bingo halls", lamenting the closure of smaller clubs. It's all a matter of perspective: many of us regretted the loss of cinemas to become bingo halls in the 1960s, but this form of recycling no doubt helped to keep fine buildings occupied and now they're once more under threat. The website tells me that the period from 2005 to 2010 was a "savage one for club closures", with the smoking ban and government-imposed changes to prize pay-outs and numbers of gaming machines.

Anyway, I'm here now and looking for action. I'm greeted by friendly staff and, as I'm a virgin, I have my own host, Tish, who is going to set me up. You can tell it was a theatre by the slope of the hall. It's smartly decorated inside, and the main auditorium is laid out in tables of four. There's an extensive arcade of what I think are still called fruit machines, a bar and a raised stage for the caller. The capacity looks about 400 to 500 and there's about fifty playing this evening, mainly women, and predominantly older, though there are pairs of girls as well as young couples. Tish is going to sit with me until I get the hang of it. She tells me that Saturday afternoons and evenings and Sunday afternoons are the busiest times. She's worked here for eight years and others have been here much longer; staff turnover is low.

They don't call, "Two fat ladies, 88" or anything like that anymore, if they ever did. It's straight numbers. And there are different types of game; in some we're competing with other players across the nation for bigger prizes, which is exciting. Everything's electronic, or it can be if you want your own pad, or whatever it's called, to note each number called while you chat or tuck into your scampi and chips.

You win some, you lose some, as they say. Though not in my case. Not a sausage, bugger all. Not that I'm bitter. It's been a very low-cost evening and they're kind enough, months later, to remember to send me nice texts with special offers on hot dogs and winning lines on the diagonals.

Back at the hotel and I'm up for the local speciality, the Hull potato pattie, a battered, deep fried disc of mashed potato, seasoned with sage and onion. Wiki tells me it's commonly sold in the port towns of Hartlepool, Hull, Liverpool and Thurso, which is an interesting combination. It's described as an inexpensive substitute for fish in fish'n'chips, which sounds like chips with a side dish of spud to me.

Next morning, I head from the hotel towards the docks and the Humber where I ended the previous stage of my walk in an August heatwave. Beyond the tired looking Ice Arena, an uninviting path leads between high security fences to the port. If there are people at work here I can't see them. Ports weren't devoid of people like this in the days when Marlon Brando coulda been a contender *On the Waterfront*. Signs warn, "Do Not Cross Lock Gates when Blue Flashing Lights and Klaxons Operate" which seems like sound advice, but it means I've reached a dead end. The only way forward is across these gates and they're open to shipping, closed to me. That might have got to me on another day, a hotter day at the end of a long walk, but today is still young and optimistic. I turn back and inland past new terraced housing and return to the Humber a few hundred yards along, past modern office blocks.

There's a 2001 sculpture, by Neil Hadlock, of a family of four from northern Europe. They've left their ship and are on their way to Paragon Station to take the emigrants' train to Liverpool, thence by ship to America. An inscription informs that over 2.2 million people passed through Hull and the other Humber ports to America between 1836 and 1914. I guess it's a cousin of the "legacy sculpture", similarly dedicated to emigres to America, which I passed in a blizzard at Albert Dock in Liverpool.

Beyond the sculpture is the entrance from the Humber into a marina. On one side there's an impressive cannon, on the other a sign that reads "Welcome". Mixed messages? This is a small part of Hull's riverside that survived the WW2 bombs. There's a plaque on one of the older brick buildings in Minerva Terrace to commemo-

186

rate the SS *Forfarshire* which sailed from here in 1838 en route to Dundee but wove herself forever into the story of Grace Darling when she foundered off Big Harcar in the Farne Islands.

Knowing that my wife plans to join me at the very end of my walk and that I'll be treating her to a weekend in Hull, I'm keeping an eye out for good places to eat. There's the Minerva pub here which looks promising and, around the corner, Ceruttis fish restaurant. And there's an ornate toilet block in front of the restaurant: she'll love that. Oh no, it's me that likes Victorian urinals, I'm forgetting.

Working my way east along the Humber from Victoria Pier, I need to cross the River Hull on that sexy new footbridge to reach The Deep where I stop to buy a bottle of water. I don't intend to take risks with that Humberside sun again. Then it's an enjoyable walk along Ocean Boulevard, no less, past Victoria Dock Village, an infilling of one of the old docks. It's a pleasant development with modest, detached houses, almost all with glass porches, conservatories and balconies enjoying the view of the Humber. That's a monotone grey this morning, the far bank indistinguishable from the river, and I love it.

Features of the old dock, including a slipway and the winding house, awaiting restoration, have been retained to provide (along with some of the street names) a sense of place and a link to the area's heritage. Around the half tide basin there are three and four storey terraced blocks and a board proudly proclaiming that the multi-million-pound housing scheme, promenade and flood defence works were formally opened in 1992 by the Burgermaster of Rotterdam, who should know a bit about these things.

There's a huge Union Jack flying from a flagpole in one of the front gardens which may be related to the EU referendum. It's upside down. I'm wondering whether to mention it to the chap by the front door but something about his tattoos and shaven head is sending me a message and I decide against it. I know one shouldn't form unsubstantiated judgements but I'm content with this one.

At the end of the promenade, and before the long run of Alexandra Dock, I have a choice. The map shows what looks a good option, continuing alongside the Humber, but it seems to run out in the middle of nowhere several miles to the east, offering the daunting prospect of a morale-sapping retreat. The route inland, behind the dock, seems safer but tedious. This is where you need good signage. And it's hopeless. There's one telling me that Liverpool is 179 miles behind me, which is encouraging, but signs for the Trans Pennine Trail to Hornsea (east coast) and Liverpool (west coast) are pointing in the same direction and the one to "Ferries" points inland. None bear resemblance to my map or reality. Rather than risk ending up back on Merseyside, I opt to follow the dual carriageway east from Hull. For miles.

Passing Alexandra Dock on the land side, there's a stretch of landscaped pathway with seats, walkers, cyclists and joggers, litterbins, flowerbeds and sculpture. As I walk past each CCTV camera by the fence that separates the path from the dock a stern voice booms, "You have been detected in an unauthorised area. Please leave the area or the police will be called. CCTV is recording." Which doesn't seem friendly.

HMP Hull is on the opposite side of the road. Handy, I suppose, for all those vagrants caught on CCTV reading the *FT* or admiring the sculpture on the path. Behind all the security fencing to my right there are some proper manly things being done like ship repairs and the manufacturing of turbine blades. One of the first happenings in City of Culture involves the installation, horizontally, of a 75-metre turbine blade in Queen Victoria Square, no doubt complementing the more familiar, heritage elements of the programme by saying something about modernity and environmental sustainability. Or it could be nothing of the sort. To give a sense of scale, that's half as long again as the height of Nelson's column in Trafalgar Square. The blade came from this site.

My seemingly unending slog along the dual carriageway takes me across a roundabout and my path is suddenly narrow, overgrown and miserable, and I suspect I'm the first to use it for several years. Eventually my path gives up and I need to cross constant, fast moving streams of traffic to continue on the other side. Happily, there's a signalled pedestrian crossing next to a very unused-looking bus stop. I have the impression that vehicles are not familiar, or impressed, with the idea of being brought to a halt here and I wave nervous thanks to four snorting juggernauts.

One of Hull's claims to fame is its own phone network which remained outside the GPO monopoly and is now owned and managed by a separate company, complete with distinctive pale cream phone boxes. I pass one of these alongside the road. It's in working order and immaculate. Perhaps it's too well hidden and sufficiently remote from any possible users to attract vandalism, which could be a useful model...

This really is one of the dullest parts of my journey, past what feels like mile upon mile of business parks, car salesrooms, filling stations, with the occasional run of housing or sewage works thrown in. This is, as they say, an hour or two of my life that I won't get back.

I reach yet another roundabout, at the entrance to Saltend Chemicals Park (Park? Park??) and turn down Paull Road, one of those with no pavement which test both my nerve and the amiability of passing motorists. Saltend is BIG. Acres, probably hectares these days, of cooling towers and pipework, both shiny and rusting, and something coming out of them in clouds that I hope is benign.

I leave the road where it crosses a stream, Hedon Haven, and follow that to the wide Humber. Two anglers are taking advantage of whatever the chemical works are contributing to the stream and it's a pleasant walk after the dual carriageway – all reeds, mudflats, derelict barges, brilliant long views across the Humber, and the sound of marsh birds.

I reach the quiet Domesday village of Paull on the bank of the Humber, with its small shipyard, a few rusting hulks, church and three 19th century pubs, one of which I call into for my fix of pint and salted peanuts.

It's now a short walk to Fort Paull which has been a fortified site since the middle of the sixteenth century, the Humber and the east coast being somewhat in the line of fire from our (occasional) friends in continental Europe. Henry VIII started the thing off. Charles I inspected troops here (presumably his own side) during the English Civil War. The Napoleonic tensions prompted vigorous "new build", the fort was in service in both global conflicts of the 20th century and it was eventually decommissioned and sold in 1960.

Brian Rushworth came across the place in 1989 when it presented a sad picture of neglect and dereliction. His father had been posted here in the Royal Artillery. Having bought it, Brian and a dedicated group of volunteers set about clearing rubbish and vegetation and controlling access to the site, and after years of effort were able to open the fort to the public in 2000.

I was put in touch with Fort Paull by the owner of Fort Perch Rock at New Brighton where I started my walk back in April. The fort is set in grounds of over ten acres on the banks of the Humber and has superb views across the estuary. Within the fortification sits a fascinating, eclectic collection of military hardware and exhibits through various conflicts, with pride of place going to the last surviving Blackburn Beverley Transport Aircraft. The Beverley is enormous. Built at the British Aerospace factory in Brough that I passed earlier in my walk, it made its final flight into Paull Aerodrome just outside the village before being moved to Beverley Army Museum and, in 2005, to its present resting place. They like to tell awestruck visitors that it was tricky to fly it into the Fort: I suspect it arrived like I did, through the gate.

Fort Paull as a visitor attraction is no modern, high-tech, digital affair: just actual, three-dimensional stuff that you can climb into, walk around, grapple with and read about, and all the better for it. It's a gem but it's not a money spinner. Visitor numbers have fallen and there's a need to generate funds to fix the roofs. There are just five staff who, between them, maintain the place, cut the grass, run the shop and the tearoom. Items are donated or loaned, rather than bought. They've tried taking on work placements (troubled kids and others who might be available to assist) but, when it comes down to it, it's largely a labour of love for those who work here. I mention City of Culture, but it seems that the 2017 people haven't shown much interest in what's on their doorstep here. Why wouldn't someone want to write a new play, set in the fort? Son et Lumiere, anybody?

Today is a quiet one at the fort but I promise to be back on Sunday when they're hosting a rally of classic American cars. For now, I have a bit more walking to do to reach my bed for the night at a B&B a mile or two further along the coast, past a wetland nature reserve at Paull Holme.

The B&B doesn't do evening meals, but the owner tells me it's a short walk back past the nature reserve to Paull village where there are three pubs. I know there are three pubs because I stopped there at lunchtime and I know it's not far, but I've walked that bit already, in the daylight, and I'm buggered if I'm retracing my steps, there and back, in the dark. When I'm able to get a signal on my phone I call a taxi and ask the driver to take me to Paull. He tells me he's Slovakian. He recommends a small hotel near Hedon but, when we get there, the restaurant is closed for refurbishment and I end up at an Indian in the same village. The driver is apologetic about the extra, redundant mileage but charges me for it anyway. I'm in Yorkshire after all.

He picks me up again as arranged, after my meal, and tells me on the way back that planners have a lot to answer for. They won't give him permission for the one new house that he's after but they're happy to allow whole housing estates. I nod.

This morning, according to the news on my iPad, Hull announces its programme for City of Culture year. The City Council will be spending £100 million to get the city ready, through roadworks and improving its pedestrianisation schemes. I'll be back in Hull in a few days but first I want to finish my coast to coast walk by, er, reaching the coast.

The B&B owner tells me it's about seven miles to Withernsea, tonight's destination. Or, he thinks, it may be fourteen. He's not sure. He and his wife bought the house, piggeries and a few acres of land as derelict and converted the outbuildings to five lets, within the original footprint to satisfy the planning officers. I make my own breakfast in the kitchen provided. My toast gets stuck in the toaster and triggers the smoke alarm. I don't risk a second piece.

As I'm leaving, I notice a large sign for the Flood Alert Assembly Point in the farmyard, which is a change from the usual, and I set off along the same road with no pavement that I followed into Paull village yesterday. There are two horse riders keeping to the left side of the road, as they're supposed to do, and at almost the same pace I'm keeping to the right, as I'm instructed by the Highway Code, and the car drivers slalom between us.

I pass a house with two prominent EU flags displayed and can but admire the pluck. I pick up the South Holderness Rail Trail (the track of the old line connecting Hull to Withernsea) for a few miles which at least gets me off the road. It's a plain earth path but it's dry. Some is in cutting, elsewhere with big views of freshly ploughed fields, muckspreading operations, stubble and distant turbines. Yet again I hardly see a soul.

The weather's good for walking today; there were a few drops of rain earlier but now it's fine with a light breeze. After my experience in August of the unrelenting Humberside sun, I've brought a beanie hat with me. My wife hates this hat but she's not here. She thinks a baseball cap would suit me, from which I assume she sees me as some ageing, overweight American who actually enjoys the feeling of having something hard pressing on his head on the hottest day of the year. At least our last dog had the good taste to bark at anyone she saw wearing one, a habit which she may have copied from me.

It's getting hotter now and I'm not carrying that much water. Nor am I passing any shops. Can you die from dehydration in Holderness? Is that even a thing? I remember always being thirsty in the summer when I was little, in the park or the countryside or at the seaside. Mum had to bring crates of lemonade just for me. And I had a habit of pressing ice lollies on my forehead, which must have looked nice when it dried.

I'm doing that thing which tells me I'm feeling under duress. I start asking myself if I would be prepared to retrace my steps if I realised I'd left something a couple of miles back. How far back? How important is the thing I've left?

Would I go back two miles for a camera? Depends on what's on the camera. Ask me again in an hour's time and the answer will definitely be no.

For a watch? How I'm feeling just now? No.

To meet Steven Gerrard? Er, no. So, I must be struggling.

If Tara Fitzgerald wanted to meet up and do part of the walk with me? Er, give me a minute, I'm thinking…

I can tell I've been (a) on my own, and (b) out in the sun, too long today.

I reach the site of the old station at Keyingham. There's a smart modern house where the path ought to be and they've incorporated the trackbed and platforms into their garden, so I divert round. Extra yardage! What's wrong with these people?

At the next disused station, Ottringham, there's a house but it's the original station building. The platforms are still recognisable but almost invisible, overgrown, not picked out as a feature of the path.

I need to leave the trail in order to work my way cross country towards Withernsea on the coast. The rail line that I've been following would take me there eventually – give or take the odd missing section – but I'll be walking some of that tomorrow and I'm picking out a (hopefully) shorter, though more complicated route, via field footpaths, minor and not so minor roads. Meanwhile, it's lunchtime. This isn't park bench country, so I settle for an uncomfortable perch on the only vertical feature in the local landscape – a muck spreader. Happily, it's not moving. The sign that I'm leaning on reads "Dangerous Chemicals" and I discover that it's not just me but a few million insects that regard this as the best place in town to tuck in. "My companion opted for the soufflé de liquid manure, kissed by an aromatic lead jus with a soupcon of pesticide du jour…"

I follow a path across a ploughed field then through woodland, but the next bit has been ploughed out and is untraceable, so I improvise. Because I'm now approaching the farmhouse from the wrong, non-authorised, direction I'm feeling a little tense and hoping that I and my beanie hat can't be seen above the hedgerow. But, for goodness' sake, I'm over here by the hedge because they've obliterated the right of way: why am I the one that feels awkward? Then along country lanes with no pavements – always a favourite – to Great Newsome Farm (lots of pigs) and brewery. I can see across the fields ahead of me to the lighthouse at Withernsea which represents my first glimpse of any feature of the east coast – my destination ever since I set out from New Brighton in April. So, a landmark in two senses. I text my wife to tell her, but it doesn't seem to have the same impact on her at work in Sussex.

The public footpath is signed through the farmyard then across another ploughed field. There is little concession to the fact that a right of way runs through the field: the line of the path is discernible and has been slightly flattened after ploughing but it's extremely painful to walk on and I can't wait to reach the far hedge line. Except that it gets worse from here: the route across the next field has been obliterated by recent ploughing so I commit myself to additional mileage and scramble along the edge of the field. There's nobody around for me to grumble to so I chunter inwardly until I reach the B1362 which leads into Withernsea from the west. Well, it couldn't lead into Withernsea from the east.

The road takes me past the lighthouse. I've arranged to come back at the weekend when it'll be open. The pub where I'm staying tonight is costing me just £30, and looks it. The "facilities" are shared but so, seemingly, are the towels and I'm not carrying any of my own. There's a self-service kitchen but no milk so I'll need to go out and buy some. There's a TV in my room but nobody can find the remote, so it can't be used; no wi-fi; and there's a cigarette end on the floor outside my door, which would on its own have been enough for my wife to have checked out.

There's not much to keep me in my room so I head out for a walk at six o'clock. This is my first sight of the North Sea that I've come so far to visit. There's a pleasant beach with groynes and boulders protecting the promenade and controlling the drift of sand. The light is fading and turning pink behind me in the west. There are two big windfarms out to sea, doing their thing and not bothering anybody.

The promenade is fronted by fine old houses. I imagine some of these were once guest houses when they were in vogue. Overall, the place feels quiet as coastal resorts can be, especially late in the season and in the evening. There are three vast amusement arcades facing across "Valley Gardens" to the sea, and a bandstand, modern but shabby, with tots on the play equipment nearby.

I walk beyond the twin towers which formerly marked the entrance to a pier. Vessels of various kinds apparently developed a liking for running into the pier and succeeded in demolishing it in stages. The pier towers now display photographs of Victorian Withernsea, its beach packed with overdressed visitors all wearing hats – no baseball caps – who no doubt arrived by train. At the far end of the prom is a lifeboat station and a boat compound complete with tractors. I turn back towards the town centre, past a greenhouse with broken panes and dying plants by the war memorial, and another sunken garden with flowerbeds and bigger children playing. This is where the boating lake used to be.

I'm ready now for my fish supper but, once inside the Golden Haddock on Queen Street, I succumb to the siren call of the spam fritter and take it back to the prom to share it with the sandflies. There are lads doing wheelies on their pedal bikes in the hope of impressing girls walking past.

Karaoke is promised at the Pier Hotel but no, not even for this book. I still have standards. Many of the shop frontages are boarded up, even the one advertising tongue bars and nipple piercers. Another holiday experience I'm set to miss out on.

I walk back to my pub past the three amusement arcades as the light fails. The arcades look lively from the outside, with noise and flashing lights, but there are no customers, just bored staff and a group of boys who occasionally rush in on their skateboards and out again.

I enjoy a quiet pint in my pub before turning in. After switching out the light I hear a party starting up in the next bedroom, with music, and it's loud. Normally I would give up and read a book with my ear plugs in. But this is too loud for me to read. I switch the light off again and fall asleep. I must have been tired.

Not fancying the shared bathroom, I depart unwashed in the morning and find breakfast in town. Queen Street, Withernsea's high street, is dominated by pound shops, boarded up premises, bookies and charity shops. The Golden Haddock looks less glamorous at this time of day and last night's spam fritter is but a fond memory. I pass the Meridian Centre, advertising American Wrestling. It bears the date 1914 and looks like it may once have been the town hall.

Withernsea was, until the Beeching cuts of the 1960s, the terminus of the Hull and Holderness railway. Before the line opened, the town had a population of only 109 but it soon grew as a resort and a fine station hotel was built, later Queen's Hotel. On closure of the line the hotel became a convalescent home, unwittingly depriving me of a bed 50 years later and consigning me to my budget accommodation along the road.

My O.S. map shows the line of a "dismantled railway" (the old line to Hull) leading away from town towards the village of Patrington where I'm booked tonight. There's nothing to say there's any public access to it, and the map has it petering out ingloriously about a mile north of Patrington. The alternative is a much longer walk along the A1033 and it doesn't appeal. There appear to be two challenges – how to find the near end of the line behind the hospital, and how to cover the awkward bit between the death throes of the trackbed and tonight's B&B.

With the help of local dog walkers, I navigate across a golf course on the edge of town and pick up the old railway line. It's then a pleasant stroll past big fields with busy farm machinery. Withernsea's lighthouse remains in sight behind me across the flat countryside and Patrington's parish church (the "Queen of Holderness") comes into view ahead. As the two striking vertical features in the Holderness landscape, it seems that both are serving as beacons for lost souls like me…

As predicted, the track expires before it gets to Patrington but not before I have crawled and scrambled the last few hundred yards through scrub and across dumped sheets of asbestos. I'm now surrounded by ploughed fields and, to cover the half mile to the main road, I follow a nettle-rich bank along a field boundary until reaching a deep ditch full of nettles and other scary vegetation taller than me. I wander up and down the side of the ditch looking for somewhere to cross and eventually opt for slithering on my backside down into the ditch and up the other side, and from there onwards to the road into Patrington.

I check into a delightful B&B, early for once, clean myself up and settle down on the bed for an afternoon watching old episodes of *Yes, Minister* and *Hi Di Hi*. There's an item on the local TV news about controversial plans drawn up by the county wildlife trust for a new visitor centre at Spurn Head nature reserve where I'll be finishing my coast to coast walk tomorrow. The plans will be on display when I get there.

The B&B doesn't do evening meals, but I'm expected at Patrington's Station Hotel along the road. When arranging my accommodation for this leg of my walk, I'd been aware that the station no longer had a railway, but I was disappointed that it wasn't now a hotel either, just a restaurant. But Jess, the manager, had made very supportive noises about my trek and said she'd be happy to chat.

She's busy when I arrive, and I occupy myself with a copy of this week's *Holderness Gazette*. 2016, I read, has been a decent year for the lighthouse museum in Withernsea, with visitor numbers matching the previous year's 10,000. There's more about the City of Culture programme and about the row over plans for the new centre at Spurn Head. And this headline catches my eye: "Council to replace bent post."

This is a piece about a damaged sign in Queen Street in Withernsea – I *know* Queen Street! The story unfolds. It is believed: "The pole was inadvertently bent by a van making a delivery to a shop". So, terrorism appears to have been ruled out… There's a quote from an East Riding Council spokesperson reassuring readers that the council will be removing the post in due course and replacing it with a new post and sign. It isn't clear whether the authorities are still seeking anyone in connection with the incident, or that anybody is receiving counselling.

Jess tells me she's been at the Station Hotel for 21 years, originally as a waitress. Before that she was studying psychology and criminology at Hull University. The place is now owned by her German father-in-law which answers my question about the array of flags on poles outside. She and her husband have a newly built house behind the hotel and have retained the old platforms in the garden. When Jess isn't too busy we talk about the walk I've nearly completed.

The meal is excellent. When I come to pay, the waiter tells me it's on the house as the manager thinks my efforts deserve support. I protest but eventually settle for Jess treating me to dinner, which is really kind, while I contribute an equivalent sum to my JustGiving sponsorship pot. It's been a great evening and, by the light from my mobile phone, I eventually find my way back to the B&B.

The best breakfast of the whole walk. Many of the hotels and other places that I've stayed do the traditional full English but, when it's cooked to order more or less in front of you, it's a different thing altogether. Five star. But my host tells me she's selling up.

This should be my last day of walking. I've made it from the west coast to the east coast and I want to finish the whole thing at Spurn Point, the end of the peculiar spit of land, Spurn Head, which juts south into the mouth of the Humber estuary. My wife will be driving up to meet me there and help me celebrate, or pick up what's left of me. There's no point in arriving too early so I've left myself a fair distance to cover.

Patrington is an attractive village, well presented, well maintained. Hidden Holderness is a voluntary group founded in 2000 to research and promote the history and character of the area and there are plenty of information panels around to make the point.

I start at St Patrick's parish church, the Queen of Holderness, Grade I listed and a gothic delight. There's already a team of volunteers tending the churchyard and grounds when I arrive at nine o'clock and a helpful chap inside, happy to point things out to me, including a sign that reads, "This is England's finest village church".

It makes sense for me to head for the banks of the Humber, then follow it as far as I can towards Spurn Point. Road walking is no fun and I've developed a thing for the Humber. It's clear from the map that some but not all of the river bank is a public right of way. I've not seen that many people in my rural potterings through Holderness to challenge me and I don't think I come across as a dangerous trespasser intent on mayhem. I'm more a writer of the occasional assertive email than a chain-myself-to-a-tree kind of environmental campaigner.

Like the lighthouse at Withernsea, the spire of St Patrick's stays in view for a long time. Well, it does the way I walk. I meet a man walking two mastiffs who complains to me about incompetent vets and has a theory that you can spot the good vets as they drive old cars. I suspect he's a fan of James Herriot. I decide not to mention that my wife, who's due to join me later, is a vet, though she would definitely pass his car test.

After mastiff man, I have the estuary more or less to myself, past Welwick saltmarsh and its bird hide, and there's a middling wind off the river. This is great walking and, knowing I'm nearing the end of my trek, I want to make the most of it. To my left, the fields are huge, ploughed and newly seeded. Having sampled the docks, chemical works and agriculture of the East Riding, I'm convinced this is a land of invisible jobs. On my right, another vast horizon and beyond the marsh the sun is shining on the river. The long, long curve of Spurn Head is clearly visible ahead and my destination, at its furthest point, looks like it will keep me going for a while. It would, I'm certain, be a mistake to disturb what I wittily call my rhythm and break into a run. I'd die before I got within six miles. Keep Calm, as they say, and carry on.

Since Partington I've seen two dogwalkers, a woman on a horse, a handful of sheep with black faces and a few egrets and smaller waders. And a lot of wind turbines. Is this the only area in England where there are more turbines than people? The spire of the Queen of Holderness is still visible across the fields behind me. It's that sort of landscape.

I look forward to the car parks marked on my otherwise rather empty map where lanes marked in yellow reach down to the estuary but, when I get there, they're rubbish. No ice cream vans, no bench, nothing.

I press on to the tiny settlement of Kilnsea at the head of the spit. It's Saturday and the place is busy with bird watchers lugging tripods, serious looking cameras, telescopes and binoculars with them. I've received text messages from my wife telling me that the traffic's been heavy and she's running late. I also discover that my plan of being picked up in the car by Mrs A at the far end of the spit is not fit for purpose: the road along Spurn Head has been seriously breached by tides and storms and, although the way to the point is open on foot, my wife would need to arrive in an amphibious vehicle if she's going to deliver on our arrangement. My vision of the intrepid hiker (that's me, by the way) – stood at Spurn Point effecting a distant gaze, with grey sea, grey Humber and grey, grey sky all about him – lies, frankly, in tatters. As Mrs A is going to be late, there is technically a possibility of my walking the length of the spit, doing my gazing and thinking great thoughts, then walking all the way back again to meet her when she turns up this side of the breach. However, that's an additional four miles of walking and, to be honest, I've not budgeted for it mentally or physically. That would leave me seriously overdrawn at the bank of sod that.

It occurs to me that any failure on my part to reach the point may be construed as a breach not only of the road, but of contract. Would people who'd sponsored me to complete the walk be entitled to their money back?

I decide to walk as far as the breach so at least I can describe it if anyone's interested, and having done some of the mileage will make me feel less guilty. But first I've earned a pot of tea and a pork pie at the Blue Bell Café which currently serves as refreshment spot and information point. There are plans on display for the spanking new centre proposed by the Yorkshire Wildlife Trust who manage the reserve. On my way here, I walked past banners and signs clearly hostile to the idea, presumably from hard-line birders who feel they don't need their hands held. One information panel tells me that the café was built in the middle of the 19th century as an ale house and was then well over 500 yards from the North Sea. It closed in a derelict state in 1991 and, such is the continuing shift in the coastline in these parts through action by the sea and the river, when it reopened as a small visitor centre in 1995, it was just 190 yards from the sea. It's not much more than half that distance now and the Kilnsea village square lies inconveniently 300 metres out to sea.

I walk down the spit, past bird scrapes and hides, and call in at a temporary information point in a shipping container, staffed this afternoon by a young trainee ranger employed by the wildlife trust. This is the kind of work I've been involved with throughout my career and it's no surprise when she tells me that, with her degree in environmental biology, she receives training and expenses but, as yet, no salary. This work is clearly rewarding in everything but money.

Not far beyond is the breach. The road just disappears and even the beach itself will be under water when the tides and wave action say so. You'd need to pick your times carefully even to walk to the end of the spit. With the sea to one side of me and the Humber on the other, this is a good vantage point for thinking about lost towns. I've always been a sucker for things that used to be but are no longer. I'm not thinking of my hair or the New Seekers so much as abandoned villages or old railway lines or stations, including those on London's Underground. Or former football stadia – did you know you can still see where Third Lanark used to play? Well, *The Legendary Lost Town of Ravenser* is my kind of book (Phil Mathison, 2015).

Much of England's North Sea coast has undergone a good deal of erosion over the centuries, continuing to this day. Historic ports like Dunwich have been lost to the sea and Spurn Head has had its own "now you see it, now you don't" settlements, notably the once proud port of Ravenser Odd, built on sandbanks at the mouth of the Humber estuary. For around a hundred years from the middle of the 13th century until it was destroyed by storms, Ravenser returned its own members to parliament and was a more important port than Hull further up the estuary. (I love this stuff.) "The Bard" clearly knew of the place and, as Ravenspurg, it puts in several appearances in three different Shakespeare plays.

I'm indebted to Mathison for the knowledge that Ravenser was granted the medieval jurisdiction rights of *infangthief* and *outfangthief* – but not *that* grateful. And I'm delighted to read of one Robert Rotenheryng, local resident and shipowner: if I'd been a mate of his at Ravenser Rotary, a bit of surname-based ribbing might have made a nice change from the usual light pillaging of Grimsby across the water.

Mathison's research concludes that, what with all the cycles of erosion and rebuilding of the spit that have taken place since, it's likely that the site of the former town lies not under the sea like Dunwich but more or less beneath the current spit or slightly to the west in the mouth of the estuary.

I turn back towards the café, following the low sea cliff. And yes, I can see another big wind farm out there. I hang around in the Blue Bell Café until it closes, when I'm shunted outside to wait for my lift. It's cold by the time my wife arrives from Sussex, but it doesn't seem wise to complain. While there are two of us, there's an opportunity to take the odd photo to mark the end of the walk. I adopt my "stare into the middle distance and look pensive" pose on the beach as my wife snaps away, to the mild interest of passing walkers and birders who probably don't view me as the kind of fashion model they're used to seeing amongst the dunes. I trail a scarf lightly in the sand to suggest abandon and moodiness and pout a little.

We drive back to Hull. It's taken four days for me to walk here from Hull and less than an hour to get back. I try not to think too hard about that.

We check into the Royal Station Hotel. This is my third stay in just a few weeks and my wife's first, so I play the "trust me, I'm a regular" card and we head for the nearest curry. Paul and Vicki, former work colleagues, husband and wife, from our Manchester days are checking in too. Paul went to university here and they're keen to revisit the place and help me celebrate finishing the walk. And there's a voucher for a big jug of Pimm's awaiting me at the bar, a "well done" from friends Helen and Phil who supported me all those months ago beyond the Pennines. This is the kind of friendship I can appreciate. It's going to be a good weekend.

On my walk I arranged to call in at various places of interest but a small number of them simply refused to be open at the right time. One was the Lighthouse Museum at Withernsea, and Paul, Vicki, my wife and I head there the next morning. It's lively and comfortingly traditional in its approach and covers local history, the coastguard service, the Royal National Lifeboat Institution, and – the reason I'm here – the life and career of actress Kay Kendall. (I think KK was probably OK with being an actress rather than an actor.)

Kay Kendall, surely the most famous native of Withernsea, was born a few doors along the road from the lighthouse in 1927 in a house which now bears a plaque marking that event. Early in her career, Kay had a lengthy romance with actor Sydney Chaplin, son of Charlie. She also had affairs with a Swedish prince, grocery heir James Sainsbury and, reportedly, with the future Prince Philip – though he may have forgotten by now. At the time of her death she was married to actor Rex Harrison.

She starred in a number of mainly lightweight comedy films of which *Genevieve* in 1954 (co-starring Kenneth More, John Gregson and Dinah Sheridan and reviewed by the *Catholic Times* as "unsavoury...smut"), was surely the best known. She was described as having "more allure in her eyes than Marilyn Monroe has from top to toe" (*Picturegoer*, 1954). Of her professional experiences in Hollywood she decried, "These extremely low-cut dresses you see out here... I wouldn't like to feel the only way I could get a man to notice me was with a plunging neckline." (*The Brief, Madcap Life of Kay Kendall*, Eve Golden).

Kay Kendall died from leukaemia at the age of thirty-two. Her memorial service in London was a star-studded affair with Alec Guinness, Terence Rattigan, Julie Andrews, Cecil Beaton, Ralph Richardson and Douglas Fairbanks Jnr amongst the congregation. Vivien Leigh addressed those present: "No one was ever born into the world with such a bright genius for living...with such intensity and gaiety did she take every minute of her stay on earth." Which wasn't bad for the girl from Withernsea.

In 1987, Kay's sister, Kim, bought the then redundant Withernsea lighthouse to create a lasting physical memorial to Kay and the volunteer run museum now boasts a pleasant little tearoom and a modest but steady flow of visitors to see a 20-minute video, film posters, family photographs, her wedding dress, costumes and accessories from her movies and a not-as-bad-as-I-expected wax figure. There are clearly many ways of getting out of the house and making a small contribution to the community if you have a few hours free, and you like old handbags.

One of the best remembered images of Kendall is from *Genevieve,* where Kenneth More's inebriated love interest plays an impromptu trumpet solo. As it happens, Kendall was miming (yes, it's true!) to a soundtrack of Withernsea's second most famous native, jazz trumpeter Kenny Baker. Honestly, what were the odds?

The views from the top of the lighthouse have been described as breathtaking. After walking up the 144 steps I have no breath left to take.

With eyes on the clock we turn towards Hull, taking in en route a return visit to Fort Paull. I was here on Wednesday for a good look around and a chat but today there's an event on – a gathering of a Yorkshire club of Classic American Car owners. It's good to see the place busy but it's now late afternoon and some of the vehicles are lining up to leave. There's just time to take in some of the permanent exhibits that I missed last time, like the gruesome hospital. Paul is as happy as a pig in…well, you know…and has to be prised out of the fort about an hour after everyone else has left.

We all head back to Hull and enjoy a fine banquet of fish, chips and mushy peas in the Minerva pub on the waterfront. By now I'm feeling like a pig in you know what myself.

Before checking out of Hull, though, I've arranged to visit the 2017 City of Culture team based in the old town. I've followed them on Twitter throughout the year, seen the changes taking place in the city centre, been in touch with potential volunteers and contributors to the programme – and had the benefit of the taxi driver perspective. But I'm keen to hear more about the driving forces behind the initiative, the expectations, community buy-in and hoped-for legacy.

The idea of a UK City of Culture, based on the European Capital of Culture model, is quite a new one. Derry/Londonderry was the first in 2013 and, to be the second, Hull came out on top of a bidding list of around a dozen, including some unfamiliar cities like East Kent, and an eventual shortlist on which Hull was joined by Dundee, Leicester and Swansea Bay. The resource implications of making a bid and hosting the year-long programme are somewhat smaller than for the Olympics or World Cup so it's perhaps surprising that more names weren't in the hat.

"Why", I ask Jon Pywell, Hull's City Culture and Place Manager, "did Hull bid to be UK City of Culture?"

The answer, it appears, was to use cultural regeneration as an impetus to economic revival – much in the way that Liverpool did from being European Capital of Culture in 2008, or Margate is doing with its Turner Contemporary gallery. The aim, Jon tells me, is for the city to become a world class visitor destination and, in the process, to create more than 1,200 jobs in the cultural sector or the visitor economy over the next ten years.

With regard to "buy-in", Jon refers to sixty artistic commissions based across different communities and the intent that there should be a high-quality arts, culture and heritage programme over the next 10 to 20 years. Hull residents will receive personal invitations to events in 2017 and it's a full programme of concerts, shows, plays, exhibitions, talks and other happenings. Over 3,200 people applied, from all wards in Hull, to become City of Culture volunteers. The tourism body, Visit Hull and East Yorkshire, has led a successful training programme aimed at all those who meet and greet visitors and residents to events – including taxi drivers.

I know, from contact made through my blog, that one *Amelia in Hull* has launched her own blog with a clear and positive emphasis on the city and its year in the "cultural sun", her aim being to tell as many people as she can what's happening and why they should visit. If that's not a bit of community buy-in, I don't know what is.

I wish them all well and look forward to revisiting Hull both during and beyond City of Culture.

I began my journey in the spring on Merseyside, an area I've been connected to all my life. I've walked "from sea to shining sea" and finished on Humberside, spending several days in and around Hull. And I love both of them: Liverpool, home of the Beatles, Billy Fury and so many other giants of the music scene; Hull, home to, erm, David Whitfield and Ronnie Hilton...

I've travelled on the Mersey ferry, on a ghost train and by narrow boat through the Pennines. I've walked – my, how I've walked – and despite my grumblings each day as the step counter ticked away, it's proved a brilliantly rewarding experience. I've attended a liquorice festival in Pontefract, a Super League game in Castleford, a gathering of brass bands in Saddleworth, a whole assortment of museums and theatres, Edwardian swimming baths and a wildflower centre (in Liverpool!). I've been made welcome at the finest cat hotel in Dewsbury or anywhere else, at a bingo night in Hull and a pub quiz in Liverpool. I've stayed in splendid old railway hotels, hostels, welcoming B&Bs and some distinctly ordinary pubs. I've eaten more curries, scouse, spam fritters, home-made ice cream, Hull potato patties and full English than you can shake a black pudding at. There's been snow and torrential rain on Merseyside and heatstroke on the Humber. I've hung out with the Pankhursts, Elizabeth Gaskell, William Wilberforce and Philip Larkin. And Kay Kendall.

And I've visited some of the most exciting conservation schemes and heart-warming community and social projects you'll encounter anywhere, meeting volunteers and staff making huge efforts to preserve and enhance the social and environmental soul of the country – with little reward beyond the knowledge that their contributions are greatly appreciated by those who benefit from them. While public services continue to be sacrificed to the gods of austerity and tax cutting, the nation owes a huge debt of gratitude to those who unflinchingly put their fingers in the dyke and strive to stem the tide.

To all of you this tale is dedicated.

Acknowledgements

Thanks go to my old friends and colleagues who joined and encouraged me along the way, compared knee problems, stood your rounds and promised to buy the book if you were in it.

My thanks also to so many project managers, enthusiasts, campaigners and girls dressed as liquorice allsorts who warmly welcomed me and shared with me your passions: you're exceptional people, take a bow. I hope to visit many of you again soon. People like Doug at Perch Rock and Brian at Fort Paull, Leah at the Everyman, Grant of Landlife, Britt at Homebaked, Anne and Janine at the Florrie, Peter and Mary at the police museum in Warrington, David of Huddersfield Canal Society, Jack and Eddy at the Modernist Society, Barry at Victoria Baths, Judith at the Pankhurst Centre, Elizabeth at Mrs Gaskell's house, Nick at the Wooden Canal Boat Society, Marianne at Mikron Theatre, Jo and Phil at the Ings Cat Hotel, Jenny at Nostell, Margaret at Goole Civic Society, Paul at the Sobriety Project, Sue at Beverley Road Baths and Jon at Hull Council.

And to sundry taxi drivers for your unequivocal advice, thank you. I wouldn't have grasped the subtleties of Brexit or Hull, City of Culture without your help.

There were many more of you: humble apologies to those I've missed. You were all brilliant.

Thank you to Alison McGovern MP for permission to quote from her grandfather Pete McGovern's paean to his native city, 'In My Liverpool Home'.

I'm deeply indebted to Dr Helen Pankhurst for the attention she devoted to my words on her family's huge contributions to the cause of women's suffrage and so much more, to travel writer Jennifer Barclay for her invaluable editorial input, to Carrie Frey for her impeccable and thoughtful proofreading, to Claire Horsman for the excellent map, and to Helen Hart, Emily Heming and all the team at SilverWood.

And finally to my wife, Margaret, who twigged that I wasn't around but encouraged me to go away anyway. You wouldn't have enjoyed it, too much alcohol, not enough vegetables. My deepest gratitude as ever for indulging me.

Also by Steve Ankers

It's a Dog's Life for the Other Half
Published in 2014 by Mereo Books
ISBN   9781861511997
RRP   £6.99

Hilarious and eminently readable.
– Terry Jones, Actor, writer,
comedian and film director

...a word of warning before you start to read *A Dog's Life*: prepare to do one of those marathon reads that takes you from dawn to dusk. This book is thoroughly unputdownable...filled with amusing anecdotes...entertaining, enthralling and totally engaging...filled with spirit and good humour. I recommend you set aside the day to binge on this brilliant book.
– *Pets* magazine

...brimful of funny anecdotes...one of those rare books that's guaranteed to bring a smile to your face at least once a page.
– *Veterinary News*

…a funny, idiosyncratic account of his long-suffering life immersed in the world of animals…Steve tells his tales with a very light touch…the author's wry sense of humour…funny, moving, serious and utterly comic…the author draws such excellent word pictures…it's certainly a great read.
– *Sussex Living*

…from the first page this book was going to be entertaining …description of veterinary visits with his brother and his wife are hilarious.
– *Veterinary Times*

It's a Dog's Life is an amusing, sometimes tear-jerking and always entertaining story…a potential stocking filler for anyone who's ever owned or cared for an animal.
– *Viva Lewes*

Grotton Revisited: Planning in Crisis?
with David Kaiserman and Chris Shepley
Published in 2010 by Routledge

A fabulous read!
– Peter Hetherington, *Guardian* Regional Affairs Editor

This book makes you laugh with the planning system, not at it!
–John Selwyn Gummer, Cabinet minister

Grotton Revisited exposes with a biting satire and razor-sharp wit the inadequacies and inefficiencies of the planning system…this is a wonderfully funny book.
– Norman Baker, MP

...frighteningly accurate...just a few degrees off centre into plausible absurdity...full of cracking one-liners...this is a book for anybody with a sense of humour...buy this book.
– *Manchester Confidential*

...adopting myriad literary forms from local rag journalism to council minutes...a refreshing approach to an incredibly complex and usually po-faced world. If you know somebody who lives anywhere near this world, buy them this book as a present.
– *Viva Lewes*

Lightning Source UK Ltd.
Milton Keynes UK
UKOW01f2112010318
318725UK00001B/10/P